THE GREENHOUSE EFFECT

THE ANSWER

by Tim Hewat

ROSTERS LTD.

Published by ROSTERS LTD
60 Welbeck St, London, W1

ISBN 0-948032-94-4

Published in UK and Europe by ROSTERS
Printed and bound in Great Britain by Cox and Wyman Ltd, Reading
Published in Australia by Wrightbooks

First edition 1989

Contents

Also by Tim Hewat

The Comet Riddle

War File

DeGaulle File

Rolling Stones File

Advertising in Australia

The Plastics Revolution

Bridge Over Troubled Waters

The Champions

The Garryowen

The Blues

Golden Fleeces — The Falkiner Years at Boonoke

Golden Fleeces II — The Murdoch Years at Boonoke

The Intelligent Investor's Guide to Share Buying

The Elders Explosion

Introduction

The Earth Abideth Forever

Recall the blind men and the elephant: the first blind man felt the tusk and said an elephant is a spear; the second felt the trunk and said an elephant is a tree; the third felt the tail and said an elephant is a rope; the forth felt an ear and said an elephant is a piece of leather, and so on. It all depends on the data you use to reach decisions. Now consider the earth from scientific points of view. Earth scientists these days are highly specialised: petrologists study rocks, stratigraphers study the layering of rock stratas, geo-chemists study chemical processes within the earth's crust, mineralogists study minerals and so it goes on; there are super-specialities among specialists, like sulphur-isotope geo-chemists. Therefore, while the earth may be a self-consistent whole, one specialist will study it from one group of data while another looks at another range of data and both will feel they have the answers, although the answers will be very different.

What the earth needs now is a generalist.

The remarkable Englishman, James Lovelock, once described by *Scientific American* as 'an original thinker caught up in wonder' is such a generalist. We shall see that Lovelock has considerable technical expertise; but what we are interested in now is his view as an independent scientist and the fact that his researches have led him to a simple yet startling point of view which represents danger, if not extermination, for our species, *homo sapiens*.

We tend to see the earth and the animals and fishes, the trees and plants, as tools for our survival and comfort; in our view, we are at the centre and everything else must dance to our commands. Not so Lovelock — and he has a name for his perception: Gaia, which the Greeks used for the Earth Goddess. He has, as he says, 'the personal sense of a real live planet on which the living things, the air, the oceans, and the rocks all combine in one as Gaia . . . Just as the shell is part of snail, so the rocks, the air, and the oceans are part of Gaia. Gaia has continuity with the past back to the origins of life, and extends into the future as long as life persists. Gaia is a total planetary being.'

The concept of the total living organism calls for a planetary outlook or, as Lovelock says, 'it is the health of the planet that matters, not of some individual species or organisms' — like human beings! This puts our current global problems into a new perspective, for Lovelock makes this important point:

> For humans, a hundred thousand years is almost indistinguishable from infinity; to Gaia, who is about 3.6 eons old, it is equivalent to no more than three or four months. Gaia has cause for concern about the long-term decline of carbon dioxide, but the rise of carbon dioxide from burning fossil fuels [to produce the Greenhouse Effect] is, for her, just a minor perturbation that lasts but an instant in time.

The immense damage human beings have done, particularly in the last two hundred years — the abuse of land, the slaughtering of species, the unbridled procreation — have been so fleeting in the Gaia context that, if we do indeed succeed in destroying ourselves, our coming and our going will have been too brief to even register on her electrocardiogram!

But they are real enough to us, three threats:

The Greenhouse Effect
The Hole in the Sky
Acid Rain

(And one must add the population explosion; the five billion people now on earth will double inside the next century, 90 per cent of the increase coming in the poor countries of the Third World. But there is no way that people are going to be induced to stop copulating, and it is very unlikely that they will ever agree to practice contraception effectively, AIDS notwithstanding. So I'll drop this one right now.)

So far, it is the alert minority who are aware of the problems; the majority are not bothered. Dr Noel Brown, of the United Nations' Environmental Program puts it nicely: 'On the one hand, we are secular, we're sophisticated, we're scientific. On the other, we are still providential — somehow, either God will provide or Nature will take care of the problem. It very well might. But will WE survive?

The solvable problems are entirely of our own making, and our escape from them will have to be of our own doing, too, because there isn't anyone else — Gaia would just forget us as we forget last winter's cold in the nose. It is going to be a close thing. It is going to require an awareness, a concerted change of mind and mass action on a scale never even imagined before. Nothing less.

Part 1

The Dangerous Trinity

Chapter

1

The Greenhouse Effect

Let us consider our situation by starting with the most threatening — the warming of the atmosphere which, in the majority view of those who are studying it, has already started. It is a recent phenomenon, but not brand new.

The term 'greenhouse gas' was used by John Tyndall, an Irish-born scientist, in a paper in London's *Philosophical Magazine* in 1863. In the last years of the nineteenth century two scientists, Svante Arrhenius and P.C. Chamberlain, wrote about it, but raised no excitement. Professor Bert Bolin, of Stockholm University, worked on the phenomenon in the late 1960s but recalls that when he discussed it with fellow scientists they said: 'This is science fiction. We don't believe it.' By the mid-1970s, however, they were starting to accept that he was right when he said: 'We, as human beings, are emitting things into the sky which will change the climate more rapidly than it has changed naturally during the last hundreds of thousands of years.'

The crucial thing about earth from the human point of view is that it is surrounded by a blanket, the atmosphere, of which the key component — Christened by Havoisiev in 1774 'vital air' — is the oxygen we breathe. Another important factor is the atmosphere's ability to stabilise temperatures. Under the heating influence of the sun, earth's temperatures in the shade vary only from 0 to about 50 degrees Celsius with an average through night and day, winter and summer, of about 15 degrees. The moon, which is much the same distance from the sun, has no such atmosphere, so its temperatures swing from a hot 100 degrees Celsius by day to a frigid minus 150 degrees by night — and its average temperature is about minus 18 degrees. Our atmosphere keeps the surface of our earth some 33 degrees warmer, and therefore habitable.

The warming is done by rays from the sun, including the very shortest, ultraviolet rays, and the longest, infrared rays which give out the sort of heat you feel when you hold your hands out to an electric radiator. Some of the incoming rays are reflected back by clouds in the sky, and others by the sea and land, particularly snowfields and deserts. Not all those reflected back

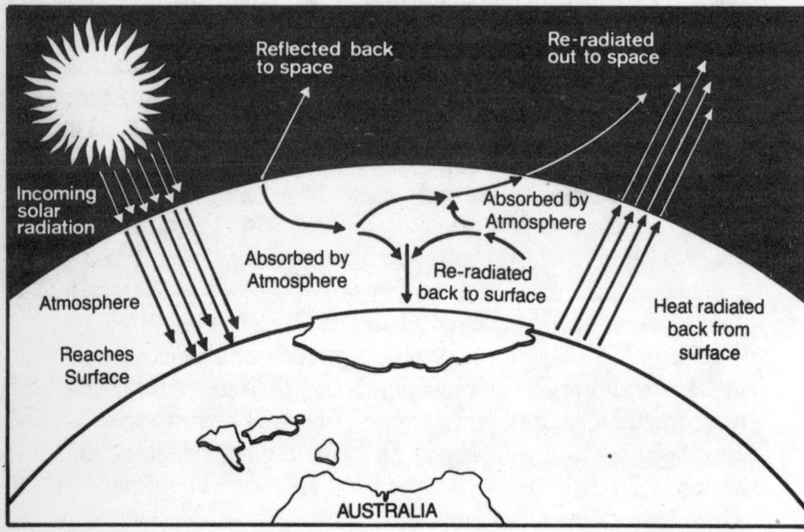

The Greenhouse Effect cycle — some heat being re-radiated

go back out into space; instead, the atmosphere re-radiates many of the infrared rays towards earth, making it warmer still. It is this ability of the atmosphere to re-radiate warm rays which creates the Greenhouse Effect.

It is important to realise that the two things in the atmosphere which catch the infrared rays in order to re-radiate them are the gas carbon dioxide (CO_2) and water vapour.

Practical thermometers were not invented until the eighteenth century; just when they were needed, because the Industrial Revolution was getting under way and man was about to start tampering seriously with earth for the first time. It is safe to assume that over the ten thousand years since the last ice age, earth's temperature remained fairly constant until the start of the Industrial Revolution. Indeed, it did not shift much coming into the twentieth century; from 1880 to 1940 there was a warming of just a quarter of one degree Celsius, but most of that was lost between 1940 and 1970; average surface air temperatures world-wide from 1950 to 1980 were 15 degrees Celsius. But things were happening.

Between 1970 and 1980 the temperature average went up by three-tenths of a degree Celsius, and first 1987 and then 1988 were the warmest years on record. Early in 1989, Britain's Meteorological Office reported that the six warmest years this century have all fallen in the 1980s.

There were, of course, those who said nothing was happening. Three scientists at the National Oceanic and Atmospheric Administration of the United States checked back over ninety-three years and reported in the first *Geophysical Research Letters* for 1989 that, as far as America was concerned, 'there is no statistically significant evidence of an overall increase in annual temperature', and Professor Kenneth Watt, of the Environmental Studies Department of the University of California at Davis, dismissed the Greenhouse Effect as 'the laugh of the century'.

But the heavy consensus of scientific opinion, robustly expressed at the international environment conference organised by *Time* magazine for its cover story 'Endangered Earth' on

2 January 1989, was clear: 'It is time to stop waffling. . . The evidence is pretty strong that the Greenhouse Effect is here' (James Hansen, head of NASA's Goddard Institute for Space Studies at Greenbelt, Maryland, and a leading expert on climate); 'We're talking about rates of climate change perhaps one hundred times faster than at any other time in human history' (Stephen Schneider, head of the climate systems group at the National Centre for Atmospheric Research at Boulder, Colorado).

Debate built through 1988 and 1989, and the world's weather really put on a circus. While the earthquakes in the Soviet Union which killed about 25,000 people in Armenia and some 300 more in Tajikistan had quite different causes, the changing weather created episode upon episode: mudslides killed 1,000 in Thailand, 75 in Papua New Guinea and 31 in Java; floods drowned more than 2,500 in Bangladesh in two onslaughts less than three months apart and 290 in Brazil, 94 in China and 8 in France, and in the Sudan some 8,000 people died of starvation following floods; conversely, millions of hectares were parched and scorched by droughts which spread across the interiors of the United States and the Soviet Union and maintained their death grip on great tracts of India and Africa; and for good measure Typhoon Ruby killed 500 in the Philippines, Hurricane Gilbert killed 65 in Jamaica and 160 in Mexico, Hurricane Joan killed 50 in Nicaragua, and Cyclone Aivu (named by the meteorologists in Papua New Guinea who watched it develop over the Louisiade Archipelago) flattened the Queensland sugar crop and associated flooding killed 8. Those were just some of the highlights.

One form of definite monitoring confirms that things are happening. By measuring bubbles of gases trapped in polar ice, scientists have shown that the amount of carbon dioxide in the atmosphere prior to the proliferations of the Industrial Revolution was about 270 parts per million (ppm). A special monitoring station established atop the mountain Mauna Loa in the Hawaiian Islands — well away from any industrial pollution — showed that by 1957 carbon dioxide in the atmosphere had risen to 315 ppm, an increase of nearly 17 per cent. By 1988, according to Dr John Gribbin, physics consultant to the *New Scientist,* it had passed 345 ppm, and *Time* at the turn of the year put it at 350 ppm; a rise in the last thirty-one years of another 11 per cent and a rise since the onslaught of the Industrial Revolution of just on 30 per cent. *Time*'s international experts further forecast that carbon dioxide would reach a level of between 500 and 700 ppm by the year 2050, a doubling inside two hundred years!

Let's see what the effects of this mushrooming are forecast to be. A fairly detailed assessment came in late 1988 from the United States Environmental Protection Agency, which spent eighteen months and $2.5 million looking at America itself. It concluded:

> Global climate change will have significant implications for natural ecosystems; for when, where and how we farm; for the availability of water to drink and water to run our factories; for how we live in our cities; for the wetlands that spawn our fish; for the beaches we use for recreation, and for all levels of government and industry.

The EPA accepted the forecast global warming, produced by several computer models, of up to 5 degrees Celsius over eighty years and said it is the speed of it which poses such danger. It was a warming of that order which brought earth out of the last ice age, but it took thousands of years and forests had time to move northward or southward to cooler climes. This time, according to Joel B. Smith, co-author of the EPA report, 'such a warming over one century would require forests to move at five times the fastest rate recorded by palaeobiologists' (biologists specialising in the ancient past). A wider study released late in 1988 by the Austrian-based International Institute for Applied Systems Analysis embraced the work by twenty-eight scientists from seventeen countries, concentrating on agricultural impact. They projected temperature rises over the next fifty years at from 1.5 to 5.5 degrees Celsius and concluded gluts would occur in most crops grown in the northern hemisphere and falls in most crops south of the equator. They were emphatic that temperature changes will be much more marked at the higher latitudes, and static at the equator, which is good news for Arctic-dwelling Canadians, Scandinavians and Siberians. Rainfall will increase, but in unpredictable patterns.

Opinion is almost unanimous that sea levels will rise — because warmer atmosphere will heat the oceans and glaciers; ice caps and parts of the polar ice will melt. (Indeed the *New Scientist's* Debora MacKenzie and Fred Pearce speculate that Greenhouse 'could leave the entire Arctic Ocean free of ice each summer within a century'.)

Over the last hundred years sea levels have risen on average about 5 inches (12.7 centimetres); a temperature rise of 5 degrees Celsius would see a further rise of about a yard (nearly a metre) and this would be devastating. The Netherlands, already below sea level, would be swamped unless existing defences could be raised dramatically; so would sections of cities like New York, London and, of course, Venice. Bangladesh (home to 100 million of the world's poorest) would vanish under the Bay of Bengal, and Pacific-island states like Tuvalu (population 8,500) would become awash. The EPA says that, even after the United States spends $111 billion on sea defences, some 7,000 square miles (an area roughly the size of the State of Massachusetts) would still be lost.

If the Greenhouse Effect is not checked, there will be some winners — farmers in the right places and urban-dwellers whose towns' climates will improve — but they will be heavily out-numbered by losers. And the Greenhouse Effect is only one of three threats.

Chapter

2

The Hole in the Sky

The partial, but ongoing, destruction of the protective ozone layer is a most intriguing problem, and a very modern one. I mentioned that the shortest rays put out by the sun are the ultraviolet rays; these are the ones which cause sunburn and skin cancers, including the often-fatal malignant melanomas. They afflict animals by causing such things as eye cancer and pink eye, and they retard crop production. A particular band of ultraviolet rays destroys the nucleic acids DNA and RNA — the basics of life. Clearly, ultraviolet rays are things we can easily have too much of. What limits our exposure?

To answer that question we must look at atmosphere in more detail. Our atmosphere is structured into four layers; the warm layer nearest earth and the one which keeps us alive is the troposphere and it has an average depth of about 11 kilometres (16 kilometres over the equator but only 8 kilometres over the poles) and it gets steadily cooler as the altitude increases; the next layer, up to about 50 kilometres, is the stratosphere in which temperatures rise with altitude; and then comes the mesosphere in which temperatures again fall, and the thermosphere in which they rise again — but the mesosphere and the thermosphere are of no great concern to us because the air up there is so thin and temperatures take on a quite different meaning.

The layer of key interest is the stratosphere, for it is here that the incoming ultraviolet rays are absorbed, in a constant creation and destruction of ozone. It is this chemical turmoil which causes temperatues to rise with altitude in the stratosphere. Why? Because chemical work is being done, and work creates heat. The ultraviolet rays crack the oxygen molecules (when we talk of life-giving oxygen we are normally referring to the molecule with two atoms of oxygen — O_2) into atoms, and the atoms reform into ozone which is a molecule with three atoms of oxygen — O_3. In turn, the ultraviolet rays crack the ozone molecules into atoms which may form oxygen again (O_2) or reform as ozone (O_3). There is a great deal of motion in this ozone layer, with gases constantly changing: the important thing is that the ultraviolet rays are being harmlessly absorbed in the process. (Oddly, ozone saves our lives in the stratosphere but is a lethal gas down here in the troposphere!)

John Gribbin, in *The Hole in the Sky,* described the ozone balance rather well:

> The usual analogy concerns a tub of water that is being filled by a tap at a constant speed, but the tub has a hole in its bottom through which water escapes at the same speed. The level of water in the tub (equivalent to the concentration of ozone) stays the same. If we make the hole in the tub bigger, the first thing that happens is that more water flows out. As it does so, the level of water in the tub drops. As the level drops, the pressure of water at the hole drops, and the flow from the tub slows down. At some point, a new equilibrium is reached, with the level of water in the tub constant at a lower level.

What is happening is that human activities are making the hole in the tub bigger, perhaps catastrophically so.

How did we learn of this menace? The story of its discovery is a fascinating one, which started with a red herring. Back in the 1960s when the Concorde supersonic aircraft was being developed by the British and French, it was thought that there would be big numbers of aircraft streaking around at high speeds and at great altitudes, above 15 kilometres and therefore in the stratosphere; the Russians were working on one and the Boeing people were designing a bigger and better job known as the 2707. So the National Academy of Sciences in America asked James McDonald, of the University of Arizona, to find out what impact the planes might have on the ozone layer. He used the then popular projection of eight hundred supersonic transports (SSTs) in service and calcualted that their jet engines would reduce ozone concentration in the stratosphere by 4 per cent — noting that a reduction of just one per cent was likely to let through enough ultraviolet rays to trigger up to ten thousand cases of skin cancer in the United States alone every year. Of course only a handful of Concordes have flown, and all other SSTs were abandoned, but McDonald's report of 1970 alerted people to the sensitivity of the vital ozone layer.

Our attention returns to the brilliant James Lovelock, Fellow of the Royal Society, who is an absolute whizz at designing and making the most sensitive measuring instruments, such as those capable of picking up gases in the atmosphere not at parts per million but parts per *trillion*. He was not actually concerned about ozone; instead he was interested in spray cans and their propellants, chemicals called chlorofluorocarbons and known popularly as CFCs. He saw CFCs as a way of mapping air currents, because the currents would carry the inert CFCs wherever they went. So he built his own gas chromatograph for 'a few tens of pounds' to measure the concentrations of CFCs at great altitudes, and he cadged a voyage on the research vessel *Shackleton* to Antarctica in the southern summer of 1971-72. Daily measurements of CFCs in tiny concentrations worked beautifully and he published his results in *Nature* — the bible of scientific discoveries — in 1973, including the premature comment: 'The presence of these compounds [CFCs] constitutes no conceivable hazard.'

Sherwood Rowland, Professor of Chemistry at the University of California at Irvine, was not so sure. He had heard that

Lovelock's measurements suggested that all the CFCs ever made — for spray cans, for use in refrigerators, and for both static and car air-conditioners — were still floating about in the atmosphere because they were chemically bound so tightly that they were almost indestructable. So what could happen to them? With his assistant Mario Molina, who had just secured his PhD, he sought to find out. They quickly confirmed that nothing happened to CFCs in the troposphere; they ultimately percolated up into the stratosphere. And here the stage was set for drama. Elementary chemistry told them that the CFCs would come under ultraviolet attack and that single chlorine atoms would be liberated from the molecules. No great drama in a few chlorine atoms floating about, is there? Indeed there is. Molina looked up the known chemical chain reactions and saw that ozone and chlorine were notoriously attracted to each other, resulting in a single chlorine atom being capable of destroying many thousands of ozone molecules. (By 1987, Rowland had worked out that one chlorine atom in the stratosphere would smash 100,000 molecules of ozone before being re-shaped itself, probably into a molecule of chlorine (Cl_2).

Rowland and Molina published in *Nature* in June 1974 but their report — which, with hindsight, was a clear warning that the ozone layer was imperilled — caused few ripples and received no attention outside the scientific community; the only dramatic action was taken by Rowland's wife who, upon being told of his findings, threw out every spray can in their home.

Nothing really happened for eight years. Joe Farman and his team in the British Antarctic Survey were working in the southern spring of 1982 at Halley Bay in Antarctica, measuring gases in the atmosphere. Indeed, measurements had been taken regularly at that base since the International Geophysical Year (IGY) of 1957. The readings they started to get made them distrust the old spectrophotometer they were using; for it said that the amount of ozone in a column of atmosphere immediately above them was way down, in fact down by 20 per cent on earlier readings over many years. Being a good scientist, and therefore cautious, Farman decided not to publish anything but to return to Halley Bay in 1984 when a new, more sophisticated measuring machine would be available. (He was additionally cautious because he knew that the Americans were monitoring ozone concentrations in the stratosphere from the weather satellite Nimbus 7 which had been in orbit since 1978.)

The 1984 readings were even more dramatic: ozone was down 30 per cent from its traditional levels; it looked as if a spring hole was developing in the ozone layer over the south pole. Farman and his colleagues published in *Nature* in May 1985, and nowhere was the impact greater than at NASA's Goddard Space Flight Center which was in charge of the Nimbus monitors. How had they failed to detect the ozone fall-off? The readings transmitted from Nimbus went into a computer for processing; the computer was programmed to throw out any wildly sub or abnormal readings, and this it had done. Fortunately the original data had been kept and, when examined, confirmed the drastic fall in ozone (which tells us yet again that computers are only as good as their programmers!)

The NASA people, although somewhat red-faced, responded very well; they set about promoting and then organising, for the southern spring of 1987, what became known as the Airborne Antarctic Ozone Experiment which had direct costs of more than $10 million and as much again in development costs. Research people from six nations became involved. The base for some twenth-four experimental flights over Antarctica was the southernmost city in the world, Punta Arenas in Chile. The scientists arrived in August and the tests spanned September and October using two aircraft: a converted DC-8 airliner carrying masses of instruments and up to forty scientists and flying crew; and a research version of Lockheed's notorious U-2 spy plane which, with a sole pilot and instruments packed in pods under the wing, went up to 20 kilometres high in Antarctic skies into air so thin that the three pilots who flew it in turn were at considerable risk.

Only days after the experimental tests were concluded, Bob Watson, the head of Airborne Experiment, announced that yes, indeed, there was a hole in the sky and, yes, it was caused by

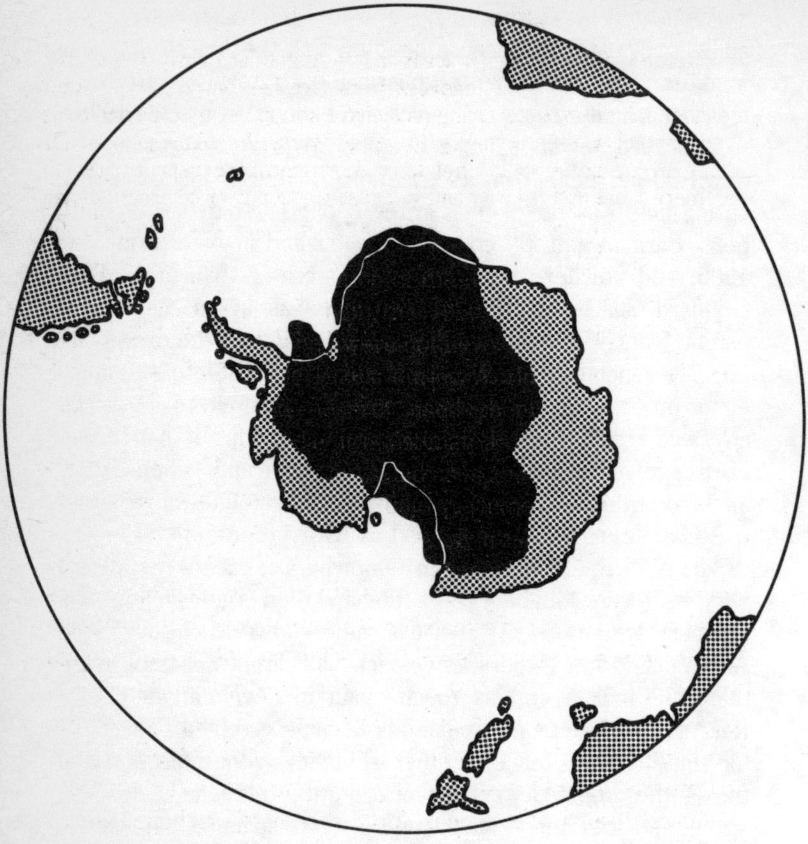

The Hole in the Sky — in October 1987 when the hole in the Antarctic ozone layer (black) covered an area the size of the United States

CFCs. The scientists still had a lot of data checking and calculating to do — work which usually takes months or years before being made public — but because of the huge importance of the threat to people of all nations, they attended a workshop in Berlin in November 1987 where they were joined by such 'hole pioneers' as Lovelock, Rowland and Farman. John Gribbin, the science reporter, attended as an observer and wrote later:

> Ozone is destroyed chemically in late August and early September each year, and then recovers from October onwards . . . And, although a dynamical change may have set up the special conditions which allow the chemistry to get to work, the consequences for Antarctic ozone would not have been anywhere near as great if there were not a large and increasing amount of chlorine getting into the stratosphere as a result of human activities, especially the release of CFCs to the atmosphere.

A curious thing is that, even though ozone concentrations over Antarctica build up again during summer, the hole itself can move! That hole of 1987 was detected over the city of Melbourne from the 11th to the 13th of December 1987, when ozone levels dropped by almost 12 per cent, letting through increased flows of ultraviolet rays to afflict the high proportion of the city's beach-going population that particular weekend. The hole, to greater or lesser degrees, was detected over Macquarie Island (between Australia and Antarctica), and the southern capitals of Western Australia and Tasmania as well as Melbourne. In fact, Tasmanians are susceptible to melanomas; the incidence among males in the decade to 1988 having almost doubled, moving from 7.9 per 100,000 to 15.2. World experts assembled in Hobart in May 1989 to try to find out why; another puzzle, put by Professor Terry Dwyer, is why there is double the number of melanomas at the same latitude in the southern hemisphere as at the same latitude in the northern hemisphere.

The hole over Antarctica was actually smaller in the spring of 1988, but this did not surprise Joe Farman, who has studied the hole and its causes since he first discovered it. His research suggests that there is a strict two-year cycle, with greater depletion of ozone in the odd-numbered years, such as 1989, than in the even-numbered years.

There is now widespread belief among climatologists that depletion of the ozone layer could be spreading around the globe. A program similar to that mounted over Antarctica was conducted over the Arctic in January 1989, with aircraft flying north from Stavanger in southern Norway. The early sorties failed to find any clouds in the polar stratosphere, but as the weeks unfolded and the aircraft penetrated nearer to the north pole, ozone depletion was indeed detected. This was confirmed by the international walking party of the northern spring of '89 which suffered serious sunburn problems. At a quite different level, measurements taken in the atmosphere above Arosa in Switzerland for more than fifty years show a decline of ozone concentration since 1970, amounting to a significant 4 per cent.

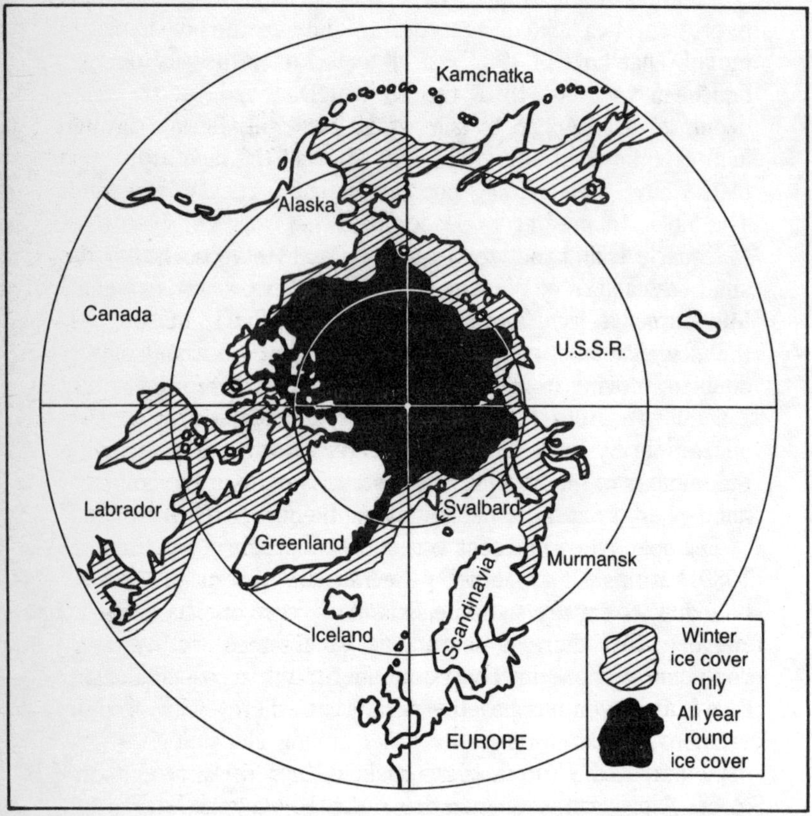

The Arctic ice waiting to be melted

Chapter 3

Acid Rain

The precipitation causing the wholesale killing of lakes, trees, fish . . . and people . . . is named, aptly, for its principal components — sulphuric and nitric acids.

The London pea-souper fog, or smog, of December 1952 hung over the great city for nearly a week; a pall of sulphurous stew. It killed more than 4,000 people, and doctors said it was the build-up of acidic particles which did most of the damage. I remember that smog well, not least for an absurd episode: I hailed a taxi in Fleet Street and asked the driver to take me to Prunier's in Lower Regent Street in the West End. But, of course, his lights could not penetrate the gloom and I was obliged to walk in front of him, outside the cab one could see a few feet and he could see my back. So thus we went in procession past the law courts, up the Strand, across Trafalgar Square and eventually to the restaurant where, with proper ceremony, I paid him off!

But acid rain is no laughing matter. In 1900 anglers took 30,000 kilograms of salmon from the seven main rivers in southern Norway; since 1970, not one has been taken. Hundreds of lakes throughout Scandinavia are now fishless; so are many of the lochs in Scotland, and it is estimated that 20,000 of the 100,000 lakes in the United States are also fishless. In the Soviet Union's Volga-Caspian basin, source of most of the world's best caviar, the sturgeon population is being devastated. And what about trees? In West Germany some 9 million acres of forests are dead or dying; in East Germany 6.4 million acres; in Czechoslovakia 2.4 million acres; in France, on the other hand, only 12,000 acres have been seriously damaged, and another 75,000 acres are showing signs of deterioration.

The term acid rain was first coined by Robert Angus Smith — from the city of Manchester in the industrial north of England, a fitting place to research the subject — in 1872 when he published a 600-page book on it; a work which was hugely ingored. So, too, was the work of Dr Eville Gorham, a Canadian academic who updated Smith's findings in the 1950s.

It was not until a Swedish oil scientist, Svante Oden, reported in 1967 a pattern of increasing acid precipitation that the scientific community started to take notice, perhaps because he termed it 'chemical war' but more likely because the real onslaught of acid rain was getting under way throughout Europe and across North America.

The starting ingredients are the sulphur dioxide and nitrogen oxides which belch up into the atmosphere when coal, oil and wood — the fossil fuels — are burned; world pumping of sulphur dioxide every year exceeds 100 million tons! British scientists from (again fittingly) the Manchester University's Institute of Science and Technology have recently established from their experimental base atop Great Dun Fell, the highest peak in the Pennines, that when these gases go into clouds hydrogen peroxide is the crucial catalyst in turning them into sulphuric acid and nitric acid, and in due course — often having been blown hundreds of miles across frontiers from where they started — they fall as acid rain or acid snow to pollute the land, lakes and rivers.

It is not actually the rain itself that kills the fishes or makes trees shed their leaves or needles; what happens is that the acid

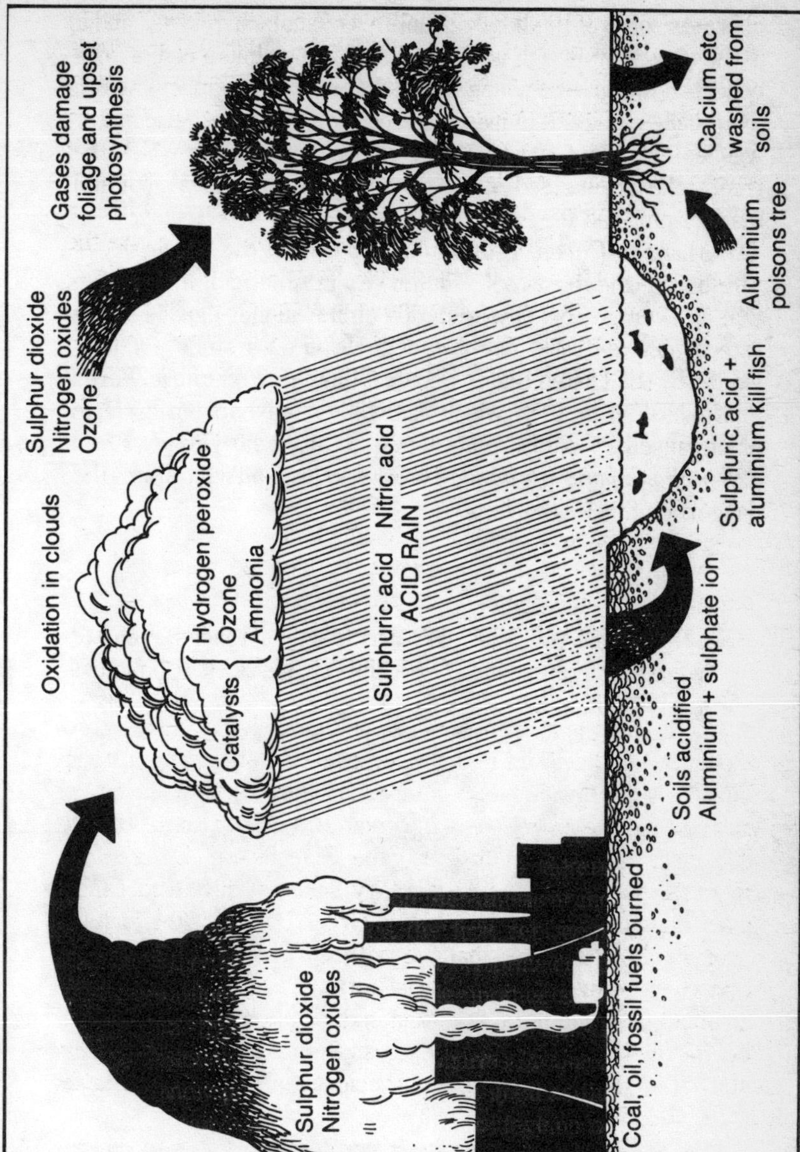

The Acid Rain cycle — from chimneys to dead trees and poisoned lakes

liberates some of the heavy quantities of aluminium in soil and it is the aluminium which is the menace — aluminium compounds collect in the gills of young fish and they exude a mucus which eventually clogs and denies them oxygen. Similarly, acid water washes nutrients out of soil and releases aluminium which the trees take up, instead of life-giving nutrients like calcium and magnesium, and they starve to death!

Bernard L. Cohen, Professor of Physics at the University of Pittsburgh (the most coal-polluted city in America), has written that an average coal power station emits sulphur dioxide at the rate of *one ton every five minutes.* He cited a study commissioned by the United States Senate Committee on Public Works and published in 1975 which said that releases from a single plant caused *25 deaths, 60,000 cases of respiratory troubles and $25 million in property damage every year!* a good indicator of the dangerous times we live in.

* * *

So, three time bombs are in place as we approach the end of the twentieth century and the ticking of the clock is only just starting to be heard.

Chapter

4

Ignorance Is Not Innocence

There was no stopping the Industrial Revolution once James Watt patented his steam engine in 1769; it powered the dark satanic mills. But perhaps the greatest mischief-maker was Sebastion Ziani de Ferranti, the Liverpool-born electrical engineer, who launched wholesale generation of power for widespread distribution more than a century later. It was 1891 at Deptford in south London when he turned on the world's first full-blown power station for the London Electricity Supply Corporation which sold its power through sub-stations to light much of the great city. Ferranti was only twenty-seven when he finished building it — he had patented a new form of dynamo before he was eighteen — and in due course his initiatives were recognised when he was elected a Fellow of the Royal Society.

It was from his example that all those stinking coal-burning monsters have been spawned; today there are literally thousands of them spread all over the globe. The figures for just one are frightening enough: every ton of coal burned produces four tons of carbon dioxide, plus heavy doses of nitrogen oxides and the dangerous sulphur dioxide. It is the carbon dioxide which is the key factor in the Greenhouse Effect, and we have seen how its volume in the atmosphere has grown — from about 270 parts per million before the onset of the Industrial Revolution to some 350 ppm today — a lift of 30 per cent.

Not all the carbon dioxide produced goes into building the Greenhouse Effect. About half of it is taken up either by trees and plants when photosynthesis, triggered by the sun, turns it into organic matter, or by the sea in which the gas sustains crude organisms like plankton. The half that does go into the atmosphere represents only half the total gases promoting the warming of the earth.

As the diagram opposite shows, carbon dioxide accounts for 49% of the gases involved, 14% are specific CFCs F-11 and F-12 (of which more in a moment), 13% a combination of water vapour, ozone and the other CFCs, 18% is methane — also known as marsh gas because it is manufactured by bacteria in swamps, in the gut of animals (huge quantities are produced in the world's fast-expanding cattle feedlots) and in termite mounds (believe it if you can, for every person on earth there are half a ton of termites) — and 6% of nitrogen oxides.

It would be wrong, too, to blame coal burning for all the polluting gases. Oil is a culprit; indeed motor cars are blamed for pushing mountains of nitrogen oxides out of exhausts, although each single coal-fired power station actually emits as much of that stuff as 200,000 cars, according to Bernard Cohen. Natural gas is guilty, and so is wood. For coal, oil, gas and wood are all fossil fuels.

The massive and savage attacks on the tropical rain forests of the world complicates the wood factor. No one has the exact figures, but reports prepared recently by the United Nations Food and Agricultural Organisation and the World Wide Fund for Nature suggest that some 100,000 acres of good timber — the habitat of thousands of species — are wiped out *every day of the year*. Some of the trees are felled and the logs put to good use, but the majority are put to the torch in huge, intended bushfires, lit by expanding populations hungry for land. This

GREENHOUSE GASES AND GLOBAL WARMING

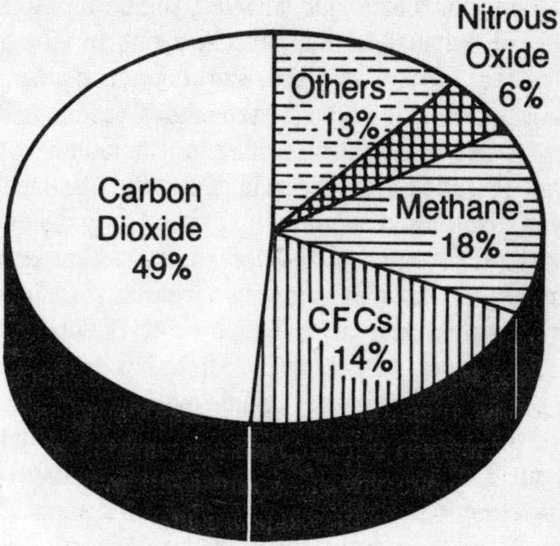

means that 4.5 million tons of carbon emissions go up into the sky from burning tropical forests every day, according to *Time*'s Environment Conference.

The Brazilians are the biggest burners by far, and they do it with guns in their hands. The deep inland provinces of Acre and Rondonia, which blanket the headwaters of the Amazon, are still going up in smoke and people who try to stop it — like Indian rubber tappers and ecologist Francisco 'Chico' Mendes — are murdered; the BBC's *Panorama* reported eighty-three murders to date. Early in 1989, three visiting American Senators were dismayed to see bulldozers in position to carve out a 'backdoor' highway from Acre into neighbouring Peru, across the Andes to Lima where logs will be shipped to Japan, the place where the finance is coming from! Second to Brazil comes Indonesia, then Colombia in South America, the Ivory Coast in

Africa, and Thailand where more than 350 villagers were killed in November 1988 by logs, which had been felled illegally, crushing down on them on a sea of mud after torrential rains.

Even if the developed countries could get their act together sufficiently to really reduce fossil-fuel emissions from power stations, factories and motor vehicles, the benefit to the atmosphere would be just about cancelled out by the intensified burning of rain forests in Third World countries.

It is sulphur dioxide and nitrogen oxides produced by burning fossil fuels that so often form acid rain. The fault is compounded by the fact that they are vented high into the atmosphere by tall chimneys, resulting in them being carried long distances, often over frontiers. (Smoke stacks 1,000 feet — 305 metres — high are common on Britain's one-hundred-plus power stations; there are more than twenty which reach 1,000 feet and two hundred taller than 500 feet in the United States, and the daddy of them all is a 1,250-feet giant over a nickel smelter at Sudbury, in the Canadian province of Ontario, which alone belches out 2,500 tons of sulphur dioxide every day!) Prevailing winds make some people winners and some losers. Much of the acid rain originating from the industrial cities of Pittsburgh, Chicago, Detroit and Toronto is decanted onto New York, Boston, Ottawa and Montreal. (Los Angeles, on the other hand, makes its own smog.) Across the Atlantic, Scandinavia and Norway in particular are the sorry recipients of acid rain created in Western and Eastern Europe, particularly in East Germany where the fuel is brown coal, low-grade lignite. (Brown coal burned in the La Trobe Valley of Victoria makes Gippsland the most polluted area of Australia.) Britain is a serious offender, too; the Environment Committee of the House of Commons estimated in 1984 that more than a quarter of the 5 million tons of sulphur dioxide belched each year from British chimneys carried across the North Sea to fall on foreign fields. Friends of the Earth reported that 14 per cent of Sweden's acid rain originated in Britain, and 7 per cent of both Norway's and West Germany's. Ontario, despite its smelter at Sudbury and the smoke stacks of Toronto, is so fed up with receiving American acid rain that late in 1988 the provincial government joined north-eastern states of the United States in filing a legal action against the Environmental Protection Agency in Washington for what the *New Scientist* described as its 'persistent denial that pollution from America's heartland in the Midwest damages the Canadian landscape'. (Canada's national emblem, the maple leaf, may vanish; many stands of maples have been so hit by acid rain that they no longer produce maple syrup.)

The entire population of the developed world became assassins of the earth from the 1950s when spray cans came into universal use. They were not new. The first spray can was used in Norway in the 1920s; during World War Two troops fighting in jungles and deserts used them to ward off flies and mosquitoes. Today it is estimated that every person living in a developed country buys and uses about ten spray cans a year to apply so many things: from perfume to underarm deodorant; shaving cream to hair spray; air freshener to cooking oil; paint to leak sealer, and even a drying agent to help start the car on damp mornings. In the United States alone, some 4 billion spray cans are bought annually!

It is not the cans themselves which are the worry, but the propellants which make them spray out the contents as an aerosol mist. The lay name for them — created by their biggest manufacturer, Dupont — is freons, but they are CFCs: chlorofluorocarbons, with atoms of chlorine, fluorine and carbon. When first developed they were used in refrigeration, both home fridges and industrial plants; they were superbly suited for it, having a low boiling temperature and being chemically stable, non-toxic, non-inflammable and cheap to make and store. Their very lifelessness made them useful cleansers of electronic circuits because they did not attack the plastic upon which chips were mounted and, later, they were used to blow foams — everything from the foamed hard plastic used to dispense Big Mac hamburgers to the foam in fire extinguishers. But, from the 1950s, it was as the propellant in spray cans that they had their biggest and most dangerous use.

It is from spray cans that the most CFCs are released into the atmosphere, although this is being challenged by the amount used in motor car air conditioners, the gases escaping both during services and when the vehicle is finally scrapped.

The crux of the problem is not simply that the chlorine in CFCs attacks and destroys the ozone layer but also that CFCs are so stable that they are virtually indestructable. Certainly nothing in the troposphere can touch them, and after they percolate through to the stratosphere, where the ozone is, it is estimated that, of the two most-widely-used CFCs, Freon-11 survives for some 75 years before being broken down and Freon-12 for 110 years! It is this longevity which makes something of a joke of the otherwise commendable efforts in recent years to limit emissions into the atmosphere of CFCs, both to save the ozone and limit the boost which CFCs give to the Greenhouse Effect. For, if not one more molecule of CFC was released into the atmosphere (an absurd proposition), the millions — yes, millions — of tons of the stuff already there is likely to last a very long time, some of it right through the twenty-first century and into the twenty-second!

Chapter

5

There are Plenty of Answers

Many say that we can dispense with fossil fuels; the world can be driven by the renewable energies: solar power; wind, wave and tidal power; plant power and even geothermal power tapped from the hot rocks below the earth's surface. The big trick is to generate electricity because electricity makes the world work — it was Christopher Joyce who wrote in *New Scientist* that a good title for a history of electricity would be *101 Ways to Boil Water.*

Some of these alternative energies have been very attractive for many years, and most of us have neighbours who have ventured along the solar route by putting a converter on their roof to let the sun heat their bath water — commendable and earth friendly. But the professionals have given up on the sun. The *New York Times* reported in March 1989:

> Some of the biggest backers of solar energy in the U.S. are losing interest . . . The world's largest maker of solar cells, ARCO Solar, is on the auction block because the parent company, which once saw its investment as a hedge against future shifts in the energy market, now believes it can put its money to better use where it

has the most expertise, in oil and gas . . . ARCO follows the Exxon Corporation and the Shell Oil Company in leaving the solar business.

The academics are doubtful, too. Bernard Cohen writes that his colleagues in the field 'say frankly that the public's expectations for solar power are highly unrealistic. They see its future as a *supplement* to other technologies.'

The trouble lies in the cost — quite apart from the climatic problem that half the time there is non-productive darkness and even the hours of potential sunlight are often cloudy or foggy or whatever. The sophisticated little devices, about an inch in diameter, which convert sun into power are called photovoltaic cells and are still quite expensive; yet thousands and thousands of them are required to produce mass electricity. Cohen estimates that to match the output of a normal power station, photovoltaic cells would have to be spread in a circle of five miles diameter to cover a total area of nearly twenty square miles. To be sure, the cost of solar power is coming down; in America it has dropped from $50 a peak watt to $5 according to Gus Speth, of the World Resources Institute; but it will not be competitive until it goes down to $1, and that last $4 will not be easy.

Hydroelectricity and wind generation are solar power once removed; water to drive hydro power stations was rain which, in turn, was water vapour evaporated by the sun, and winds are the result of the sun's uneven warming of the atmosphere. On the face of it they are both clean sources of power which produce no wastes. But most of the world lacks the rivers and terrain to run hydro plants, and wind generation calls for large numbers of propellers atop poles which, again, means wind farms covering big tracts of real estate. (A successful exception can be seen on the sweeping grasslands of Inner Mongolia where — according to Paul Gardner, a British engineer who spent a year in Sinkiang province testing wind turbines for the Chinese — 'tiny 100-watt wind turbines charging truck batteries have become so popular with the nomad herdsmen as a means of providing power for lighting and television that even production of 15,000 machines a year cannot meet demand.')

In Britain the government supported wind research, but the output was very small; a 1-megawatt wind turbine came into commission on the Kent coast in 1989 and a pair of new generators — one a vertical axis 500-kilowatt machine and the other a 330-kilowatt horizontal unit — were approved for the test site at Carmarthen in south Wales. However it cut off support for a scheme to harness wave power, although a group of private engineers kept advocating the enclosure of large areas of open sea (off Lancashire, Lincolnshire and Sussex) with barrages equipped with turbines and sluice gates so that power could be generated on both the ebb and flow tides — getting power coming and going! The fact is that a lot of these lovely ideas are quite impractical because electricity has to be available when users want it, not when the elements can generate it.

Much less fanciful is the work in the biomass area in which re-growable plants are the source of fuel. This was foreseen at the turn of the century by Rudolf Diesel, who conceived and built the first diesel engine in 1897; he wrote.

> The diesel engine can be fed with vegetable oils and would help considerably in the development of the agriculture of the countries which will use it. This may appear a futuristic dream, but I can predict with great conviction that this use of the diesel engine may in future be of great importance.

Quite so. A man in accord with Diesel is the American professor Melvin Calvin, a great authority on carbon dioxide (and, therefore, the Greenhouse Effect) whose brilliant biochemical work on photosynthesis won him the Nobel Prize for chemistry in 1961. During the oil crisis of 1972 he found himself in his car at the end of a long queue for gasoline, and as he waited he realised how stupid it was to be sitting in line to buy the fuel of dead fossils when there were dozens, indeed thousands, of living plants which could produce equally good fuel and go on doing so year after year. On their own ranch in northern California, Calvin and his wife found several such plants, including the gopher plant which produces combustable latex very much like that in the rubber tree, *Hevea brasiliensis*. The Diamond Shamrock oil company confirmed that the oil from living plants could be cracked catalytically to produce efficient oil and proceeded to invest in trial plantations — as did many others, including the Japanese.

All the renewable energy sources have potential, some better than others. But so far their production is piddling, incapable of doing anything to assuage the earth's affliction or meet the ever-growing appetite for energy. Years down the track they may be marvellous; but we do not have years.

The fastest improver is actually the arch-villain itself, coal. All power stations are inefficient; they realise only a fraction of the punch the basic fuel carries. Now the drive is to lift efficiency, and thus lower the amount of fuel burned for the same result. To this end the Tennessee Valley Authority in the United States has built a commercial-scale boiler using the newest (and tongue-twisting) technique of Atmospheric Fluidised Bed Combustion (AFBC). The boiler at the Authority's Shawnee plant at Paducah, Kentucky, is thirteen stories high with an area of 2,160 square feet — it is a big vertical boiler to produce generating power for 160 megawatts. Into this tall column is fed a mixture of crushed coal and limestone which fall to a base perforated by 9,000 air-blowing nozzles designed to keep the mixture swirling while the coal-dust burns. (The heat from burning turns water into steam to drive the turbines, as in any other power plant.) The coal gives off sulphur dioxide as it burns, but instead of this going out up the chimney it is absorbed by the limestone. The plant is said to be 15 per cent more efficient than the old coal plants and, because nitrous oxide is also trapped, it does not contribute to the acid rain problem and its part in the Greenhouse pattern is reduced by 90 per cent. The British are going down the same track, but they substitute 'pressurised' for 'atmospheric', hence PFBC instead of AFBC. British Gas and Osaka Gas of Japan are joint-venturing an $8 million project to squeeze gas from coal (burning gas is not nearly as polluting as burning coal), and the Japanese are developing a vast network of in-company (including business complexes, hospitals and hotels) mini-generators serving a smallish area in a more efficient way — it is called 'cogeneration'.

All kinds of schemes are being explored to make power generation more efficient and much cleaner. But development, testing and then widescale adoption are slow, taking many years and, as we said earlier, the world does not have years.

Chapter 6

The International Players

Many of the world's politicians agreed in the late 1980s that a clean-up had to be achieved on a world-wide basis. It was a rare burst of mutual understanding, refreshing to observe.

Certainly some nations had been quicker than others to realise that world-saving measures had to be taken. Way back in 1978 the American Congress legislated to make CFC-driven spray cans illegal although, of course, the Americans had been far-and-away the biggest makers of CFC cans; the Canadians also banned them and so did the Swedes. In 1980 the United States Environment Protection Agency moved to limit the manufacture of CFCs for all uses including refrigeration; but Reagan succeeded Carter the following year and — not surprisingly for a man who told lobbyists for California's forests when he was governor: 'If you've seen one Redwood, you've seen 'em all' — killed the project. But the United Nations Environment Programme (UNEP) picked it up and, with the slowness typical of the world bureaucracy, succeeded in getting twenty countries to sign the Vienna Convention for the Protection of the Ozone Layer in March 1985. It was not much more than a pious statement of hope, but it did lead to what is known as the Montreal Protocol. This is an agreement signed by twenty-seven of the thirty-three countries which sent delegations to Montreal in the autumn of 1987 which binds them, from the start date of New Year's Day 1989, to steadily reduce the release of CFCs in stages; by 20 per cent by 1994 and by a further 30 per cent by 1999 (base year 1986). As later forecasts have shown, it was a pretty weak effort; but it was a start, and it happened before the wider population had woken up to what was going on up there in the stratosphere — first reports of the Antarctic flights confirming the Hole in the Sky were not released until a fortnight after the Protocol was signed.

The next twelve months saw a great awakening, sufficient to alert politicians everywhere that there could be votes in trying to save the earth! An unlikely hero emerged: the imperious Margaret Thatcher, of whom *The Economist* said: 'That most hard-headed and urban of politicians has become deeply interested in the sort of environmental issues that ten years ago would have made her snort with irritation.' *New Scientist*, never a fan of hers, wrote that 'Mrs Thatcher walks with her head in the ozone layer', while the *Herald* in Melbourne wrote about her conversion 'from hard-line free enterpriser to swooning greenie' — which suggested they do not know the lady very well; she has never been known to swoon.

Late in 1988 it was Thatcher who sent out invitations — 'this is re-cycled paper' — asking world leaders to join her at a Save the Ozone Layer conference in London in March 1989. One hundred and twenty-three of them turned up to hear her say: 'It is not a case of some countries asking other countries to act, it is a case of every country taking action . . . No one can opt out.' Prince Charles gave reinforcement in an after-dinner speech to delegates in which he said: 'Part of the problem has been to convince the man in the street that unless the ozone layer is protected he won't be able to STAND in the street without wearing sunglasses and a thick coating of No 16 sun blocker — and that will just be in winter.' He added: 'The seas are fast becoming sewers. The rain forests are being turned into deserts. If we can stop the sky turning into a microwave oven, we will still face the prospect of living in a garbage dump.' And he has vowed since to heat his homes by burning clean straw instead of dirty coal! For environmental good measure word was put out from Buckingham Palace that all royal vehicles, from the Rolls Royces down, had been converted to lead-free petrol and the Queen released from her garden ten thousand balloons bearing the message: 'I love lead-free'.

In the event not everyone accepted Thatcher's dictate that 'no one can opt out'. The world's two most populous nations — China with well over a billion people and India with nearly a billion — would not have a part of it. They argued, with a good deal of justice on their side, that the developed nations caused the damage to the ozone layer; so, if they wanted the poor nations to help them repair it, they must pay the bill. (Currently China produces less than a tenth as much CFCs as the United States but, under a plan to put a refrigerator in every house by the end of the century, it will come up to match American production.) China's spokesman at the ozone conference was Liu Ming Pu, vice-chairman of his country's Commission for Environmental Protection; he told delegates:

> The developed countries have produced global problems of grave magnitude. They took advantage of cheap energy in the past to accumulate wealth, which they can now use to manage the environment. The developing countries face expensive energy costs and so cannot accumulate wealth to protect the environment.

His solution? To establish an International Ozone Layer Protection Fund, paid for by rich nations, to find substitutes for CFCs and to pass on the know-how to signatories of the Montreal Protocol. The Indians extended that with the suggestion that the Fund could be used to compensate chemical companies and manufacturers for the free transfer of the know-how to poor nations; their minister for environment and forests, Ziul Rahman Ansari, saying:

> The technology of substitutes, conservation, re-cycling and equipment modification will be almost wholly the monopoly of a few companies in the developed world . . . The question that haunts us is the extent of resources required to get the technology as well as the products from the companies in the developed world.

Eventually another twenty countries agreed to sign the Montreal Protocol, lifting the membership of committed CFC-cutters to fifty-one, and a dozen more said they were thinking about it; but roughly half the countries attending remained unconvinced, or uncommitted. (Ironically, Brazil was among the Montreal joiners, but less than a week later passed a resolution in company with the seven other member-countries of the Amazon Pact denouncing world pressure to save the rain forests and then, in another flip a month later, Brazillian president José Sarney — while loudly proclaiming '*A Amazonia e nossa*' (The Amazon is ours) — announced a $100 million, five-year plan to develop the area properly and 'monitor environmental activities.' As the *New York Times* reported 'ecologists immediately condemned the program as inadequate' and it was doubtful whether the Brazillian parliament would even pass it into law!)

Mrs Thatcher had the last word, not simply by giving the closing address to the conference but by announcing that Britain would double its annual contribution to the United Nations Environmental Programme to some $2.6 million; she also gave a timely serve to Britain's refrigerator makers by advising people not to buy new ones 'until ozone-friendly ones are available'.

Just four days later another international meeting — not attended by Thatcher and 80 per cent of the nations which had turned up to *her* conference — opened at the International Court of Justice in The Hague under the leadership of Holland, France and Norway to discuss the Greenhouse Effect itself. Although short, the line-up included such heavy-weights as King Hussein, Presidents — Mitterrand, Mubarak and Magabe, Chancellor Kohl and Prime Ministers Carlsson, Gonzalez and

Mulroney. They came up with a startling idea for a new institution called Globe which they promoted by publishing 'simultaneously in major newspaper around the world' under the heading 'Declaration of The Hague', dated 11 March 1989. It said, in part:

> Because the problem is planet-wide in scope, solutions can only be devised on a global level . . . The signatories acknowledge and promote the following principles:
> A) Developing, within the framework of the United Nations, a new institutional authority which, in the context of the preservation of the earth's atmosphere, shall be responsible for combating any further warming of the atmosphere . . .
> B) That this institutional authority undertake or commission necessary studies, be granted appropriate information upon request, ensure the circulation and exchange of scientific and technological information — including facilitation of access to the technology needed — develop instruments and define standards to enhance or guarantee the protection of the atmosphere and monitor compliance herewith . . .
> C) Promote the effective implementation of and compliance with the decisions of the new authority, decisions which will be subject to control by the International Court of Justice . . .

It was a bold, possibly silly step to think in terms of a new world authority (Mrs Thatcher and others immediately poured cold water on it), but it showed again that the message was getting through: the world needs help. Other international groups at that time were active: the twelve countries of the European Community met in Brussels and agreed that they would all reduce CFC production by 85 per cent and go for a total ban on them by the end of the century; President George Bush responded by calling for a total phase-out in America, too, by the year 2000. The United States was not as happy with a global conference of 116 countries at Basel in Switzerland, which worked on a treaty to control exports of dangerous wastes — Greenpeace has estimated that between 1986 and 1988 more than 3 million tonnes of waste were shipped from industrialised nations to third world countries. The Americans objected to several clauses, and were not among the first 35 countries (including France and Canada) to sign on the spot.

Other steps were taken on a national or local-government level. For instance, Britain — according to environment minister Nicholas Ridley — had assurances from its spray-can industry that CFCs would not be used after the end of 1989; 'as those aerosols currently constitute 60 per cent of the CFCs used in the United Kingdom, by that means alone we shall have achieved our Montreal Protocol objective by the end of this year', he said. Further, Chancellor of the Exchequer Nigel Lawson — in what was described as the Thatcher government's third 'green' budget — lifted the tax differential between un-leaded and leaded petrol by 4 per cent, making un-leaded about tenpence a gallon cheaper than leaded at the pump.

In the United States more than a fifth of the states passed laws to bring in compulsory re-cycling programs covering newspapers, bottles, plastic containers and much more; Jeanne Wirka, a solid-waste analyst for Environmental Action in Washington, told the *New York Times*: 'I think the whole waste issue is going to bring changes for manufacturers and especially for consumers.' Certainly things started to take dramatic form in Los Angeles where the citizens' love affair with the automobile knows no bounds. By a vote of 10 to 2 the directors of California's south coast air-quality-management district — a regional agency with authority over Los Angeles — adopted a twenty-year anti-pollution plan which will not only cut the use of cars but will see nearly all vehicles converted to 'non-polluting fuels by the year 2009.' The 'L.A. Plan', as it is called, is concerned with more things than cars; in the first five years regulations will ban spray-can deodorants and hair sprays and oblige companies to install the best anti-smog devices regardless of cost. But the car was the prime target, as *Time* reported on 27 March 1989:

> The plan's primary objective is to break the city's addiction to the internal-combustion engine. First, it imposes stricter emission standards and forces employers to encourage car pooling. Then it calls for conversion of most vehicles to methanol and other cleaner-burning fuels. Finally, in a Buck Rogers phase that assumes rapid

advances in fuel-cell technology, it calls for a massive switch to cars, buses and trucks powered by electricity.

Additionally, the California Air Resources Board ordered that from 1993 refineries must produce cleaner-burning diesel fuel, cutting its sulphur content from the present average of 2.8 per cent to 0.05 per cent, a measure likely to cost truckies at least 11 cents more per gallon. In West Germany the government, working with local authorities and manufacturers, moved to halt the dumping of CFCs in the two million refrigerators and freezers scrapped by Germans every year; all citizens have to do is telephone their local waste disposal authority and arrange for the units to be collected and taken to a network of central depositories for the safe removal of CFCs — cost: just a few Deutschmarks.

In Australia, with an Ozone Protection Act in place, Prime Minister Hawke — whose Labor government had earlier refused $1 million for Greenhouse research — flip-flopped by announcing an $8 million energy research program, winning editorial praise from *The Australian* for pointing out 'that nuclear power generation, which does not use fossil fuel, is therefore made even more attractive' — a notion which immediately outraged his more left supporters.

All this reforming zeal is bound to translate into big bucks for some entrepreneurial manufacturers. Not surprisingly, du Pont — biggest manufacturer of the dangerous CFCs with annual sales of some $750 million — determined not to lose the business; early in 1989 the American chemicals giant announced that it had patented the first replacements for CFCs, one of them having lost the crucial chlorine component to become simply a fluorocarbon (FC) while another added hydrogen to become a hydrochlorofluorocarbon (HCFC). The firm's alternative-development manager, Charles McCain, acknowledged that the new propellants were not as good as the old ones and would in many cases require users to develop or buy new machines to handle them; indeed, du Pont estimated that the banning of CFCs renders useless, or requires alteration of, capital equipment valued at $135 billion in the United States alone, and McCain added: 'It is going to be difficult to develop all the substitutes by the turn of the century.' Those that were trying included General Motors, American Telephone and Telegraph, Northern Telecom of Canada, ICI in Britain (who entered into joint ventures to develop substitutes with du Pont), and in Japan NEC and Matsushita — Matsushita had been using an astonishing 3,800 tonnes of CFCs a year to clean the electronic circuit boards it makes (Not to be outdone, McDonald's, the American hamburger king with franchises all over the world, including China, announced that it would find an 'environment friendly' pack to replace the CFC-containing polystyrene boxes in which it sells its notorious Big Macs!)

It is hard to think of a time in history when so much thought, talk and action is being devoted to a single set of problems; maybe World War Two saw such a concerted effort, maybe now is the first. Therefore the reader must find it strange, if not remiss of me, that I have made hardly a mention of the mighty source of energy which is efficient, which is clean, which is statistically safer than crossing the street and which does not threaten the earth.

Logic dictates that nuclear power can lead the crusade to save the earth.

Part

2

Super Energy's Time has Come

Chapter 7

What a Hell of a Way to Open

Lieutenant-colonel Paul W. Tibbets, commander of the United States Air Force's 509th Composite Group based under the shady palm trees which lined the long airstrip on Tinian, an island near Guam in the Marianas, had piloted his B-29 Super Fortress Enola Gay for nearly 1,500 miles through the summer night. As the hour hand of his watch edged up towards eight o'clock on the morning of 6 August, 1945, he headed his high-flying aircraft over the island of Shikoku and the band of Inland Sea which separates it from Hiroshima, an ancient military city of nearly a million souls on the main Japanese island of Honshu. At eight o'clock precisely, Tibbets had Enola Gay immediately overhead Hiroshima at 30,000 feet and the bombadier working behind him released one bomb, containing Uranium-235 as the explosive material, set to go off when it fell to an altitude of 2,000 feet above the teeming city. Within sixty seconds some 80,000 people were dead and, as the United States Atomic Energy Commission reported later, every building within a radius of half a mile of the explosion was razed and light damage was sustained over an area of about two hundred square miles.

Sixteen hours later the White House in Washington — presided over by Harry S. Truman who had so recently succeeded the mightly Franklin Delano Roosevelt — put out a press release which said, in part: 'That bomb had more power than 20,000 tons of TNT . . . It is an atomic bomb. It is a harnessing of the basic power of the universe. The force from which the sun draws its power has been loosed against those who brought war to the Far East.'

Three days later bombadier Kermit Beahan, in another B-29, released a plutonium-powered atomic bomb on the port of Nagasaki and killed some 40,000 more people. Within a week the god-emperor Hirohito and his generals had laid down their samurai swords and surrendered. World War Two was over.

The atomic bombs made a sensational debut as far as weapons of war are concerned. But so horrific was their impact and so threatening their potential that they gave nuclear power a lousy name before its civilian use was even launched. No great source of energy has ever arrived with such appalling advance notices.

And it was, in fact, a long time coming.

It started with a genius called Ernest Rutherford who could hardly have come from greater obscurity; he was born in the village of Brightwater in Nelson Province in the South Island of New Zealand. But at the age of twenty-three he won a scholarship which took him to the famous Cavendish Laboratory at Cambridge University (he later became the Cavendish Professor of Experimental Physics and director of the laboratory). His early work on radioactivity won him a Nobel Prize for chemistry in 1908 (and he was knighted in 1913 and became a lord in 1931). It was in 1919 that he, with Frederick Soddy at Manchester University, made the discovery which opened the way to nuclear power via fission, the division of the atom; by bombarding nitrogen with particles from disintegrating radium, he changed part of it into an isotope of oxygen. When Soddy realised that Rutherford was switching atoms from one element to another, he exclaimed: 'This is transmutation.' Rutherford's response: 'Don't call it transmutation. They'll have our heads off as alchemists.' This did not, as Spencer Weart has told us in *Nuclear Fear*, prevent Rutherford from waltzing round the laboratory singing *Onward Christian Soldiers* with gusto.

The work was expanded by the British scientists Blackett, Cockcroft and Walton, and at the University of California at Los Angeles Ernest Lawrence built the so-called atom-smasher, the cylotron. In Rome in 1934 Enrico Fermi split the uranium atom but did not recognise that he had done so! So it was left to the German radiologist and director of the Kaiser Wilhelm Institute for Chemistry, Otto Hahn, working with his assistant F. Strassmann to complete the picture. They reported in January 1939 — just eight months before the start of World War Two — that by bombarding uranium (with an atomic number of 92) with neutrons they had obtained an isotope of barium (atomic number 46, far removed from uranium), they had split the nucleus into two parts — atomic fission had not only been achieved but had been observed to have been achieved. Just three months later the Paris-based trio of Jean Frederic Joliot, Hans von Halban and Lew Kowarski reported in *Nature* that their atom-splitting experiments showed that, in theory, a chain reaction was possible — and that is precisely what an atomic bomb is, and so is an atomic power reactor.

A sharp reporter on the *Sunday Express* in London, one C.A. Lyon, picked up the report in *Nature* (read then, and still today, largely by the scientific community) and his editor splashed it across the front page under the headline 'Scientists make an amazing discovery' for the millions to read over morning tea on 30 April 1939: 'A discovery of such terrific potentialities that it may transform the world beyond man's wildest dreams is being investigated in the laboratories.' Lyon quoted one unidentified scientist as saying that the potential power was 'too great to trust humanity with.'

With world war about to start, one is entitled to think that all national leaders would want to know much more about the 'amazing discovery', and quickly. But they reacted coolly.

Indeed, Winston Churchill, who quickly replaced Neville Chamberlain as Britain's wartime Prime Minister and proved most successful in the role, was worried that stories of appalling new weapons which could wipe out cities in seconds could damage morale among his forces and population. The French, however, did take steps to secure the only known supply of heavy water, needed to develop chain reaction research. Jacques Allier, a secret service agent, was sent to Norway to buy the stuff. But the German Gestapo were after it, too. After many adventures Allier and the water returned to Paris shortly before the Germans invaded France. This time the scientist Joliot and his colleagues moved the water in secret and stored it in the condemned cell of the prison at Clermont-Ferrard. But it was still not safe, so they put it aboard a coal barge bound for England, where the water was stored first in the Wormwood Scrubs prison and later in Windsor Castle!

If the politicians were not too interested in atomic power, the scientists certainly were. And an odd circumstance arose: it was the brilliant Jewish scientists who fled in the late 1930s from fascist persecution in Hitler's Germany and Mussolini's Italy — Albert Einstein, Enrico Firmi, Leo Szilard and Niels Bohr who went to America, and Otto Frisch and Rudolf Peierls who went to work in Birmingham in Britain — who addressed the potential of atomic bombs.

Albert Einstein — born in Bavaria and already a Nobel Laureate for his Theory of Relativity and other outstanding discoveries — wrote to his new President from Peconic on Long Island on 2 August, 1939, because 'it is my duty to bring to your attention the following facts'. He outlined recent work in America by Fermi and Szilard and explained:

> This new phenomenon would also lead to the construction of bombs, and it is conceivable — though much less certain — that extremely powerful bombs of a new type may thus be constructed. A single bomb of this type, carried by boat and exploded in a port, might very well destroy the whole port together with some of the surrounding territory.

He told Roosevelt that 'I understand that Germany has actually stopped the sale of uranium from the Czechoslovakian mines which she has taken over' and he urged the President to appoint a permanent contact between 'the Administration and the group of physicists working on chain reactions in America', Einstein's suggestion fell on deaf ears.

William Laurence, the extraordinarily capable science reporter for the *New York Times*, who had heard Fermi talk about chain reactions at a meeting of the American Physical Society at Columbia University, was also aware that the Germans would be working on it and spent months gathering and checking material. His report appeared on the front page on 5 May 1940 under these headlines:

VAST POWER SOURCE
IN ATOMIC ENERGY
OPENED BY SCIENCE

Relative of Uranium Found to
Yield Force 5 Million Times
as Potent as Coal

GERMANY IS SEEKING IT

Laurence received no reaction from his government. So, sure that his warning was important, he re-wrote his story and it appeared in the widely-read magazine *Saturday Evening Post*, again to no obvious response — although five years later he learned that it had been classified as 'secret' by defence bureaucrats who have little or no comprehension of mass circulations.

Across the Atlantic the embattled British government was somewhat startled to receive from Frisch and Peierls a typescript of three pages, headed: **'ON THE CONSTRUCTION OF A SUPER-BOMB** — based on a Nuclear Chain Reaction in Uranium'. They wrote that they wished to 'discuss a possibility which seems to have been over-looked' in earlier discussions. It concerned the separating out of the 0.7 per cent of Uranium-235 from the 99.3 per cent of Uranium-238, the two isotopes forming uranium. They explained that the pure Uranium-235 would 'constitute an extremely effective explosive', predicting that the energy released by just five kilograms of it would be equivalent to several thousand tons of dynamite.

Action was taken and physicists went to work in laboratories at Oxford, Cambridge, Birmingham and Liverpool by mid-1940 under the unlikely code name of MAUD. Progress was kept very hush-hush under wartime conditions, the link with power and authority was through Churchill's personal scientific adviser Professor Frederick Lindemann (later Lord Cherwell). That fine historian A. J. P. Taylor has given us a splendid footnote: the crucial discovery of how to control a nuclear reaction, and thus be able to make a bomb, was made by refugee scientists who, as aliens, were 'still forbidden to possess bicycles and had to obtain special permission from the local police when they went to London to report their discovery to the government'. The report in 1941 delighted Lindemann, and at his urging Churchill ordered that work be started on a separation plant for Uranium-235. Britain, with total secrecy, was committed to trying to produce an atomic bomb.

At much the same time things started to move in the United States; Einstein wrote again to Roosevelt shortly before the Japanese attack on Pearl Harbor brought the United States into the war; this time he was heeded and by 1942 an all-out American effort to build a bomb had started under the code-name Manhattan Engineer District, later changed to the Manhattan Project. An early work site was an abandoned basement squash-court underneath Stagg Field at the University of Chicago; there Enrico Fermi and his team did indeed build the world's first nuclear reactor — and for some years afterwards a brass palque wired to a fence on the site proclaimed: 'On December 2 1942 man achieved here the first self-sustaining chain reaction and thereby initiated the controlled release of nuclear energy.'

Bomb development was pursued in the desert of New Mexico. At the Los Alamos National Laboratory in the summer of 1943, the team — including Fermi, Bohr et al — was joined by

British and Canadian scientists as a result of the Quebec Agreement between Churchill and Roosevelt; among the Britons was the outstanding Bill Penney, a shambling fellow who later designed the British A and H bombs. Anthony Sampson gives us the attractive story of Penney being drawn into a discussion of how to measure the atomic blast when the first bomb was tested near Alamogordo in mid-summer 1945: 'Why don't you try' he suggested, 'putting a row of tin cans across the desert to see how they get dented by the blast.' The bomb test and the tin cans worked spectacularly.

Then came Hiroshima.

The White House announcement included a passage which was to prove of importance, almost an omen for nuclear power, and not a good omen at that:

> It has never been the habit of the scientists of this country or the policy of this Government to withhold from the world scientific knowledge. Normally, therefore, everything about the work with atomic energy would be made public. But under present circumstances it is not intended to divulge the technical processes of production or all the military applications, pending further examination of possible methods of protecting us and the rest of the world from the danger of sudden destruction.

President Truman added this undertaking: 'I shall recommend that the Congress of the United States consider promptly the establishment of an appropriate commission to control the production and use of atomic power within the United States.'

We all know about the bombs on Hiroshima and Nagasaki. What few of us know is that by the time they were dropped, the Manhattan Project in all its manifestations had spent more than $2 billion on the development of an industry employing more than 45,000 people — all of it controlled by the Pentagon. The military were keen to keep their control, arguing that the secret of the bomb could be preserved only by them. Scientists, on the other hand, lobbied persuasively in Washington that post-war civilian decision-makers, not the military, should control nuclear weapons. Truman, a scrappy little fellow from Independence, Missouri, was always a man of his word; the Atomic Energy Act of 1946 established, as he had promised, an independent, civilian-controlled Atomic Energy Commission.

It must be said, however, that the advent of the Cold War between Russia and her former allies maintained a fairly high level of military hysteria and it was the military alone which forged ahead with atomic weapons development. The fourteen plants built in America to produce plutonium — nine of them at Hanford beside the Columbia River near Richland in Washington State and five beside the Savannah River in Georgia — each produced much more than a million kilowatts of heat energy in their reactors, but this was never used to generate electricity; it was simply looked upon as a dangerous nuisance! Further, a super application for atomic power plants was in submarines, for reactors required no air for their operation whereas conventional oil-burning engines did; *USS Nautilus*, the first launched in 1955, established all kinds of endurance and under-water distance records. Additionally, the subs' reactors needed refuelling only at very long intervals.

For eight years under the Act of 1946 only the government was allowed to build and own reactors in America. This was changed under a new Atomic Energy Act passed in 1954 and the new pattern emerged, and continues today, whereby private contractors built reactors, largely for public utilities. Consolidated Edison, which supplies New York City with electricity, announced that it was buying an atomic generating plant which Westinghouse would build beside the Hudson River, and Commonwealth Edison, supplying Chicago, got General Electric to build its first reactor; Con-Ed and GE have remained the big rivals in nuclear expansion, with boiler-makers Combustion Engineering and Babcock and Wilcox in the minor league.

In Britain the military chiefs of staff were panting for a bomb of their own, arguing over and over again that 'Britain could not afford to be left out of a field of such potential'. Clement Attlee's Labour Government agreed and atomic development remained a military matter, and a very secret one, and power generation was ignored for the time being. Dr Penney was put in charge of bomb building at a factory near the village of Aldermaston in

Berkshire. The result was Britain's first atomic bomb detonation on Monte Bello Island, just 50 miles (80 kilometres) off the coast of Western Australia above the Tropic of Capricorn, on 3 October 1952.

The people working at the atomic research establishments — Aldermaston, Harwell and so on — were segregated by secrecy, the families living right on the bases; life was pretty unreal, too, because absolutely no expense was spared and few questions asked, not least because politicians and bureaucrats could not know what questions to ask. One result was a procession of traitors: Klaus Fuchs, Alan Nunn May, Bruno Pontecorvo, scientists who spied for the Soviet Union (which had actually beaten Britian by three years in the race to explode a bomb, thanks in large part to the traitors' information).

The British governing body was the Atomic Energy Authority (AEA), established after Churchill returned to power in 1951. While its prime responsibiliey remained military, such were the power shortages in post-war Britain that the industrial use of atomic power had to be explored, too. This found expression in October 1956 near the military plutonium plant at Windscale in the windy wastes of Cumberland, just below the Scottish border; Queen Elizabeth II flicked a switch and the Calder Hall power station started to feed the first atomic-generated electricity into the national grid. *The Times* eulogised next morning:

> The colorful, and almost Wellsian-looking installation, deeply stirs the imagination . . . Truly, it has been described as a courageous enterprise; for Calder Hall represents the inauguration of a comprehensive programme of atomic power stations which, in time, will provide Britain with an ample supply of electricity without the use of coal or oil. Therein lies its magic.

These were, indeed, euphoric times for nuclear enthusiasts, and Harold Macmillan's Tory government announced that Britain would build nineteen nuclear power stations producing 6,000 megawatts of electricity by the end of 1965 at a cost of £3 billion. (The euphoria was dented somewhat in October 1957 when a fuel rod in the military reactor at Windscale was allowed to catch fire and radioactive Strontium 90 spewed out of the chimney to affect more than eight hundred farms — this was probably the first nuclear plant accident.) After a flurry during the fifties in Dwight D. Eisenhower's America, there was a lull during President Kennedy's years. Then came another flurry of activity from 1965 under Lyndon B. Johnson; by 1968 more than a hundred reactors for power stations were either ordered, under construction or operating in the United States and more than half the generating capacity on order was nuclear. Similarly France and other European nations were going nuclear, as were Japan and Taiwan. People were starting to say that all our tomorrows would be nuclear.

But . . .

Chapter

8

The Building of a Phobia

When the *New York Times'* William Laurence witnessed his first atomic bomb test in the atmosphere on Bikini atoll in the Marshall Islands of the Pacific in 1946, he was moved to report that it was 'like being present at the moment of creation when God said "Let there be light"'. Those first pictures of the bomb's extraordinary mushroom cloud in the first minutes after explosion immediately became etched in the memory of everyone who saw them. The contradictory reactions of excitement and doom at that time are described by the American writer Spencer Weart in his 1988 book *Nuclear Fear*:

> Talk of the mysterious core of atoms recalled the problem of forbidden secrets; talk of atomic energy recalled fantasies of magic power, apocalypse and a Golden Age . . . People had long been searching for mighty, life-transforming rays; now at last they had found something resembling what they sought.

Mixed feelings were compounded by fear as the Cold War between the United States and the Soviet Union intensified into the most expensive arms race of all time; atomic bombs escalated to hydrogen bombs and we all knew that large parts of our civilisation, such as it is, could be wiped out within minutes. There was another factor, as Dick Kovan wrote in the *New Scientist*: People perceived that the first atomic scientists 'were dangerous keepers of secrets of awesome forces whose terrible power they alone could control. Such an individual dabbling with mysterious powers has an ancestry that goes back to the likes of Pandora. Images of the evil or mad scientists tampering with powers beyond their control are still being brought to us in books, films, TV and radio.'

Fear and mistrust translated to mass opposition in Britain and elsewhere, in the Campaign for Nuclear Disarmament (CND). It was formed one night early in 1958 at the home of the Canon of St Paul's Cathedral, John Collins, attended by such literary luminaries as Bertrand Russell, J. B. Priestley, Michael Foot, Kingsley Martin, Ritchie Calder and A. J. P. Taylor. James Cameron, who was there and who had observed three atmospheric bomb tests, wrote later:

> In its impact on thinking people it was really not comparable to any citizens' movement in history . . . CND reasoned that the existence of the nuclear bomb, being a situation unprecedented in the experience of mankind, demanded a human reaction equally unprecedented . . . The Bomb was a fact; we did not try to un-invent it. But we argued that it was useless to meet a unique condition of threat with the old and empty responses of Balance of Power, of Spread the Risk, of Diplomatic Arrangement . . . The movement for unilateral nuclear disarment believed, fiercely and fundamentally, in Multilateral Disarmament . . . The CND people, like all rational human beings, saw total international nuclear disarmament as the principal chance for any final salvation of the species.

CND meetings were hugely attended. They were supported, as Cameron has written, by 'individual men and women of all parties and of none, from every variety of religious, social and industrial groupings, from every walk of life. It had no formal membership, but its administration was democratic and elective.' Its greatest manifestation, which for a few years was a vibrant British tradition, was the annual march from the atomic design establishment at Aldermaston to London, a trek of about fifty miles taking three days. The marchers — many of them pushing prams or, like Labour leader Michael Foot, accompanied by their dogs — trudged through country and then the London suburbs, slept at night in schools and public halls and finally filled Trafalgar Square, 100,000 strong. Foot's biographers, Hoggart and Leigh, have written the truth: 'CND was a failure. It did not Ban the Bomb... What CND did leave behind was a glow of exhilaration and then nostalgia among those who had supported its cause.'

CND had its echoing movements in America, through Europe and in Australia and, although nearly all the organisations have withered, there is the immense ongoing fear of nuclear annihilation, although most of us have learned to live with it and our fears are somewhat lightened by the emergence of Gorbachev and *glasnost* in Moscow. The pity, even the tragedy is that fear of atomic warfare has been carried over to apply to the peaceful and positive uses of nuclear energy.

It is the cleanest and most effective source of energy the world has; yet so many people have a phobia about it that projects in country after country are being shelved or abandoned. What can be the source of such a silly phobia?

As with most phobias, it is based on ignorance and that ignorance is nourished by dis-information — misleading information either purposely or carelessly put out. Nobel Laureate Rosalyn Yalow points the finger: 'The media, in collaboration with a variety of activist groups, have developed among the people an almost phobic fear of radiaton at any level'

The fear is radiation. So what are the facts on radiation? Bernard L. Cohen, Professor of Physics at the University of Pittsburgh and the author of more than two hundred papers in scientific journals, knows a good deal about radiation:

> Every person in the world is struck by about 15,000 particles of radiation *every second* of his or her life, and this is true for every

> person who has ever lived and for every person who will ever live. These particles, totalling 500 billion per year, or 40 trillion in a lifetime, are from natural sources. [Nearly everything around us — the walls of our houses, the roads we drive on — shoot out sub-atomic radiation particles which are called gamma rays, neutrons, electrons and so on at very high speeds, something like 100,000 miles per *second*.] In addition our technology has introduced new sources of radiation. By far the most important is medical X-rays — a typical X-ray bombards us with trillions of particles of radiation.

This gives the lie to the propagandists who proclaim: 'Every dose is an overdose.' And it makes a nonsense of those signs proclaiming: 'This is a nuclear free zone' It shows, too, how mischievous Sheldon Novick was when he wrote in his influential anti-nuclear book of the 1960s, *The Careless Atom*:

> When one of these particles or rays goes crashing through some material, it collides violently with atoms or molecules along the way... In the delicately balanced economy of the cell, this sudden disruption can be disastrous. The individual cell may die; it may recover. But if it does recover... after the passage of weeks, months or years, it may begin to proliferate wildly in the uncontrolled growth we call cancer.

Doomsaying Stuff. The important factor is quantity. The quantity of radiation is usually measured in millirems (though sometimes in curies, or in millisieverts). One millirem of exposure corresponds to being struck by approximately seven billion particles of radiation. Is this serious? Well the standard work on radiation is the 1975 report by the National Council on Radiation Protection and Measurements in the United States which says that people living in westernised societies absorb one millirem every four days from natural sources, or 86 millirems a year. It cites 30 millirems a year coming from cosmic rays showering down on us, 20 from radioactive materials like uranium, potassium and thorium coming up at us out of the ground, 10 from building materials like brick, stone and plaster and 25 from our own bodies, mostly from potassium, plus a total of about 1 millirem from trival sources such as rays put out by television picture tubes, luminous numerals on an alarm clock or wristwatch or a flight in a jet airplane at high altitude which exposes us to more cosmic rays. The British have assigned those 'natural sources' vis-a-vis nuclear radiation; the National Radiological Protection Board reported in 1987 that of all the radiation exposure to the population: 'Natural radiation accounts for 87 per cent; medical sources (ie, X-rays) for 11.5 per cent; occupational exposure for 0.4 per cent, and discharges from the nuclear industry for 0.1 per cent — or 1 part in 1,000'

Professor Cohen has monitored media coverage of nuclear radiation for more than thirty-five years, always alert for the reports on national television and in the newspapers to give the radiation exposure in millirems, 'but it is hardly ever given. Eventually it appears in a technical journal or I trace it down by calls to health officials; on a very few occasions it has been as high as 5-to-10 millirems, but in the great majority of cases it has been below 1 millirem'. Cohen has cited several cases of media hysteria:

> In the supposed leaks of radioactivity from a low-level waste burial ground near Moorhead, Kentucky, there was no exposure as high as 0.1 millirem, yet this was the subject of a three-part series in a Philadelphia newspaper bearing the headlines: 'It's Spilling All Over the U.S.' 'Nuclear Grave is Haunting Kentucky' and 'There's No Place to Hide'. In the highly-publicised leak from a nuclear power plant near Rochester, New York, in 1982, no member of the public was exposed to as much as 0.3 millirems; yet this was the top news story on TV and in newspapers for more than 24 hours.

A further example among many is the particularly interesting way a newspaper in Boston handled the infamous accident at the Three Mile Island power plant which after all — according to the *Report of the President's Commission* on the matter — produced average exposures in the surrounding area of 1.2 millirems; the paper put up a one-word banner headline: 'RADIATION'. Surely that showed, in 1979, that radiation was firmly established as a phobic word in the American psyche. And not only in America. Newspaper readers everywhere can recall such scare headlines. To be fair, a sound explanation was offered to a House of Lords committee by one G. Fraser, director-general of the nuclear policy division of the Commission of the European Community:

> The problem is that often the popular channels of communication have sensationalised the matter and unjustified claims have hit the headlines. Such things sell newspapers and also sell advertising because of greater circulation. Newspapers are in the business of making profits

(I am obliged to admit a contribution to the phobia: when the Windscale reactor caught fire in 1957 I was a producer for Granada Television in Britain and with great glee transported a cow from the area into the studio which, when a geiger counter was held near her udder to detect radioactivity in her milk, ticked like mad; good show business, but silly science.)

Certainly the phobia was fuelled by a handful of accidents of which Windscale was the first. With about 30 per cent of the advanced world's electric power now being generated by some four hundred nuclear plants, it is not surprising that there are a number of minor and insignificant mishaps; indeed, the United States Department of Energy reported in December 1988 a list of '155 instances of contamination at 16 weapon plants and laboratories'. (In its coverage of the report, the *New York Times* failed to make any reference to millirems in any of the incidents — instantly qualifying for a place in Professor Cohen's rogues' gallery.) But I think there have been five accidents, including Windscale, which have been major builders of public apprehension.

The second, and possibly the worst of all, came in the northern winter of 1957-8 in the southern Ural Mountains of the Soviet Union. Nikita Krushchev was coming to power and he ordered that the whole thing be kept secret; it was this very secrecy which, in the end, meant that the disaster aroused so much interest. The central place was called Kysthym; there the Soviets were dumping plutonium-contaminated waste down bore holes and it went critical and exploded. The whistle was blown first in the *New Scientist* by the dissident biochemist Zhores Medvedev, who reported that 'several hundred people'

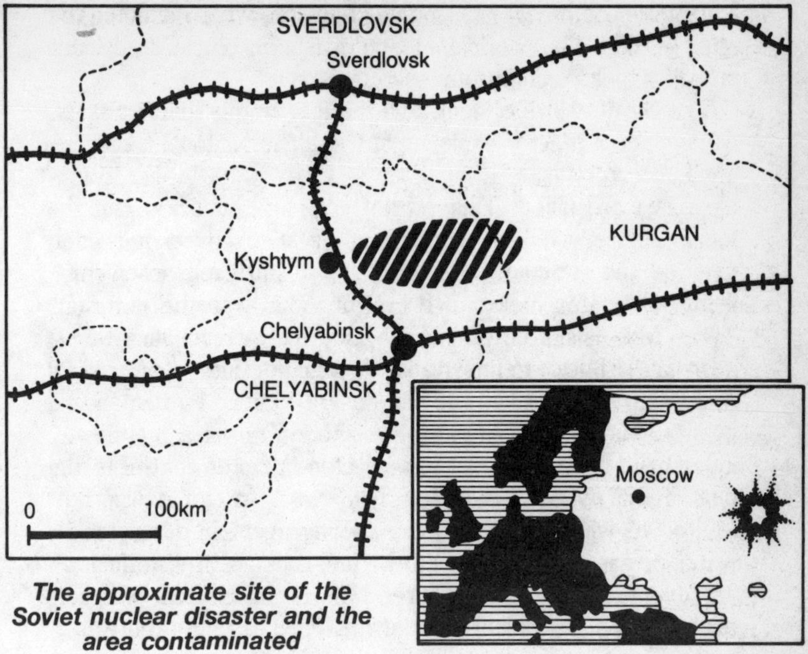

The approximate site of the Soviet nuclear disaster and the area contaminated

had died from radiation sickness after 'strong winds carried a mixture of radioactive products and soil over a large area, probably more than a thousand square miles'. Confirmation built up in a strange way: from 1958 onwards, Soviet scientists published more than a hundred papers in learned journals on the effects of strontium-90 and caesium-137 on plant and animal populations, although no geographical locations were ever given; clearly there had to have been a major disaster to provide them with data. Then, late in 1988, thirty years on, Space Media Network — a Stockholm-based company which markets satellite images and which provided first pictures and details of the later Chernobyl disaster — announced that computer-enhanced pictures confirmed that an area of 250 square kilometres round Kysthym remained abandoned; some thirty villages which were marked on pre-1950 maps were overgrown or destroyed, farm land was deserted and a river blocked, presumably to stop the flow of radioactive water. Christer Larsson, who conducted the study, said: 'The world's most devastating nuclear accident probably took place in total secrecy.'

The third major accident, and the first in the United States, came when a reactor exploded at the Idaho National Engineering Laboratory near Idaho Falls in January 1961. Three employees were killed. This did not get huge publicity. But the fourth certainly did, in part because a state governor recommended the evacuation of all children and pregnant women living within five miles of the plant. This was the notorious Three Mile Island power plant beside the Susquehanna River, near Harrisburg, Pennsylvania, which got into strife on 28 March 1979. It was, and still is, described even by responsible publications like the *New York Times* and *Time* as a 'meltdown', indeed the first meltdown in a reactor (a factor central to the plot of the movie *The China Syndrome*). In fact it was not. Meltdown will occur when the cooling agent in a reactor — water or gas — vanishes and the fuel rods are free to heat up and eventually melt. The Three Mile Island incident was certainly a Loss of Coolant Accident (LOCA); a tap in the water-cooling system remained open in the No 2 reactor when the people on duty believed it had been closed, and the water was escaping. The official inquiries afterwards speculated that if water had continued to escape for half-an-hour to an hour, meltdown would have occurred. But executives on duty — and one who had been telephoned at home — suggested closing an auxiliary valve (tap) in the pipe through which the water was escaping. That did the trick, although the reactor is still not operating. Tony Hall wrote in his *Nuclear Politics*;

> Public opinion the world over was shocked by the events of Three Mile Island. They were disturbed, too, by the way in which the public was misled about what was going on in various phases of emergency. The public acceptability of nuclear power was now seriously in question.

Ten years after the event I think one must agree with Hall. Construction work was halted on nuclear power stations throughout the United States and there was a questioning worldwide — although no one was killed at Three Mile Island and there was no significant radiation. The episode was the sort of bad luck that nuclear enthusiasts simply did not need. Nor did they need the fifth and most bizarre accident of all: Chernobyl, the experiment that turned into a disaster.

We are talking about a huge establishment standing on the bank of the Prypiat River near where it joins the Dneiper in the northern Ukraine, a location about 60 miles north of Kiev and 450 south-west of Moscow. The building where the disaster developed — housing reactors Nos 3 and 4 — had an area of 11,000 square metres, considerably bigger than a soccer pitch, and was 71 metres high — equal to about twenty-five storeys in a modern skyscraper. The adjoining hall housing eight pairs of turbines was 400 metres long by 50 metres wide, equal to two soccer pitches or sixty-five tennis courts. The adjoining town of Prypiat (population 45,000) was, as it were, a company town, with everyone working at or involved with the power station; it has since been entirely abandoned as have many other towns and villages.

The fullest account of what happened is given in *The Chernobyl Disaster* by Viktor Haynes and Marko Bojcun — a fascinating read, although stupidly and inaccurately sub-titled *An Unanswerable Indictment of Nuclear Power.* According to the first Soviet account to the International Atomic Energy Agency (IAEA) in Vienna: 'At 0123 hours and 40 seconds on 26 April (1986) an emergency occurred in the fourth unit of the Chernobyl nuclear power station during the *scheduled shutdown* of the unit while at a power level of seven per cent.' (Italics added) The way Haynes and Bojcun tell it is rather different:

> It all began . . . with an experiment. Its purpose was to improve safety — more precisely, to ensure a constant supply of electricity to the pumps that circulated cooling water around the reactor's uranium fuel rods. Should these pumps' normal electricity source — the reactor's turbine generators — fail, the water would stop circulating, and the fuel rods would overheat, melt and explode. Ironically, an experiment designed to avoid such an event actually caused it to occur.

The details are quite technical. Sufficient to say that when the operators were ready to start the experiment 'they switched off the reactor's emergency water-cooling system, to prevent it un-necessarily flooding the core and shutting down the reactor while the experiment was in progress'. Then, to their surprise, the regional grid controller in Kiev ordered that the No 4 reactor keep feeding the national grid. The experiment had to be posponed for nine hours, but 'they did not bother to switch back on the reactor's emergency water-cooling system. This was a violation of the plant's safety rules — the first of six violations they were to commit.' Violations two, three, four, five and six followed until at twenty-three minutes and forty seconds past one o'clock on the Saturday morning (just as the Soviets later reported) the fuel rods in the reactor, ferociously hot from lack of coolant, and under great pressure, disintegrated and broke through their housings to combine with the steam water. The explosion triggered by this interaction was so powerful that it lifted the 1,000-tonne, concrete-filled steel lid clean off and more explosions followed. 'A ball of fire burst over the reactor core', wrote Haynes and Bojcun . . .

> About a quarter of the 2,000-tonne core — 1,700 tonnes of graphite, 204 tonnes of uranium fuel, and tonnes of control rods, pipes and steel structures — was hurled outside the reactor vault . . . The physical destruction of the building was colossal. The reactor had become a raging inferno.

Thirty-one died in the hours, days and weeks after the explosion, many of them having shown much courage. High atmospheric pressure overhead drew Chernobyl's radiation cloud that first morning to an altitude of some 6,500 feet (2,000 metres), although some went higher into the jet stream and was carried as far as Japan. For the next eleven or twelve days, steady winds carried the clouds over much of Europe and Scandinavia, and later to Britain and Ireland, and rain on most of those days washed the particles onto land and lakes. While more than one hundred thousand Russians were being evacuated by bus from the immediate disaster zone, heavy fallout was measured in Sweden and Finland, Poland and West Germany and, to a lesser extent in a dozen other countries. (One of the sudden hysterical reactions was the subsequent destruction of thousands of reindeer in Swedish Lappland in the belief that their flesh was too radioactive to eat!)

Nearly three years later *Pravda* reported in March 1989 that nearly a quarter of a million Soviet citizens are living on land so contaminated by Chernobyl that they are receiving special food supplies to avoid over-exposure to radiation. This echoed a report a fortnight earlier by Steve Goldstein, of the American Knight-Ridder newspaper chain, that the farmers in Ukraine, Belorussia and the Russian republic itself call the 30-rubles-a-month food subsidy *na grop*, the coffin subsidy, that half of the 26,000 people in the Narodichski district 80 kilometres from Chernobyl have developed enlarged thyroid glands, and that women 'are advised not to get pregnant'.

Two facts are beyond dispute: one, Chernobyl was a mighty disaster; two, it was the result of human error, indeed a procession of human errors. This is acknowledged by Haynes and Bojcun who added: 'All the major accidents before Chernobyl at civilian nuclear plants — including Windscale and Three Mile Island — were caused by human error.' To say that is not to solve the problem; but it indicates that improvements in design and training and control procedures can address the problem and get the better of it.

Further, one must view the matter in perspective. Professor Cohen, who we met earlier, has done considerable research on the risks we run in life and published several papers including *Perspective on Occupational Risks, Society's Valuation of Life Saving* . . . and, with I. S. Lee, *A Catalog of Risks.* The measure he uses is Loss of Life Expectancy (LLE), explaining:

> The LLE is the product of the probability for risk to cause death and the consequences in terms of lost life expectancy if it does cause death. As an example, statistics [from the United States Bureau of Statistics] indicate that an average 40-year-old will live another 34.8 years, so if he takes a risk that has a 1 per cent chance of being immediately fatal, it causes an LLE of 0.348 years (0.01 × 34.8). It should be clear that this does *not* mean that he will die 0.348 years sooner as a result of taking this risk. But if 1,000

people his age took this risk, 10 might die immediately, having their lives shortened by 34.8 years, while the other 990 would not have their lives shortened at all. Hence, the *average* lost lifetime for the 1,000 people would be 0.348 years. This is the LLE from that risk.

Cohen found that one of the greatest risks in American society was remaining unmarried. Figures from the National Center for Health Statistics showed that a single white male has

Professor Cohen's Loss of Life Expectancy (LLE) Table

Activity or Risk	*LLE in days*
Being male rather than female	2,800
Heart disease	2,100
Being unmarried	2,000
Cigarettes — one packet of 20 per day	1,600
Working as a coal miner	1,100
Cancer	980
Being 30 pounds (13.6 kilograms) over weight	900
Being poor	700
Stroke	520
All accidents	435
Motor vehicle accidents	200
Alcohol	130
Suicide	95
Homicide (murder or manslaughter)	90
Drowning	40
Fire, burns	27
Firearms	11
Diet drinks — one per day throughout life	2
All electric power in U.S., nuclear (UCS)	1.5
Airplane crashes	1
All electric power in U.S., nuclear (NRC)	0.03

a life expectancy of 62.3 years versus 68.3 years for the married white male, giving him an LLE of 6.0 years, while for single white females and non-white males and females the LLEs are 3.2, 8.8 and 6.0 years respectively. He produced an intriguing table of various risks and their LLE which, with permission, is printed opposite. To the theme of this book, the most interesting figures relate to nuclear power and its risks, and Cohen adds this note on the theoretical basis *all* power in the U.S. is nuclear generated:

> According to the study by the U.S. Nuclear Regulatory Commission (NRC) the risk of reactor accidents would reduce our life expectancy by 0.012 days or 18 minutes [nearly equal to the risks of smoking two cigarettes!] whereas the Union of Concerned Scientists' (UCS) estimate is 1.5 days [or a lifetime consumption of 200 cigarettes]. Since our LLE from being killed in all accidents is now 435 days, it would be increased by 0.003 per cent according to NRC or by 0.3 per cent according to UCS. This makes nuclear accidents tens of thousands of times less dangerous than moving house from New York to California, an action taken by so many Americans with no consideration given to the added risk. Yet nuclear accidents are what many people are worrying about.

A different echo was given to the British House of Commons late in 1988 (and quoted later by Derek C. Hampson, General Manager of the Australian Uranium Information Centre) in figures of industrial deaths for the ten-year period to March 1988:

Coal mining industry	366
Offshore oil and gas installations	79
Nuclear power generation	5*
Rest of electricity production & distribution	57

*None of the nuclear deaths were related to radiation

In this The Age of Information we all know how important publicity is in creating mass perceptions; that is why corporations pay public relations consultants considerable sums of money to keep their image in good shape. Negative publicity leads to negative attitudes. With this in mind, Cohen enlisted the library of the Argonne National Laboratory to help him monitor reports in the *New York Times* Information Bank on various types of accidents over the years 1974–8. He then compared the number of reports with the number of fatalities each year for each type of accident, with the following results:

Type of Accidents	*Average stories per year*	*Average deaths per year*	*Average deaths per story*
Motor vehicle	*120*	*50,000*	*416*
Industrial	*50*	*12,000*	*240*
Asphyxiation	*20*	*4,500*	*225*
Radiation	*200*	—	—*

*Reports about radiation accidents outnumbered all the others put together, yet there were no deaths caused by radiation during the review years nor for at least ten years before that; whereas other types of accidents killed an average of 66,500 Americans a year.

Conversely, media pay little or no attention to good nuclear news. When the Spitak earthquake killed tens of thousands of Armenians in December 1988, the nuclear literate looked for news of the two power-station reactors at Medzamor, only about 45 miles (72 kilometres) from the epicentre. The dailies carried a sentence or two reporting them undamaged, but there was the usual sting in the tale in the reports put out by the news agencies Reuter and *Agence France-Presse*: 'Local environmentalists have long complained that a nuclear station outside the Armenian capital lies on a geographical fault line and was vulnerable to tremors.' Not so vulnerable, it would appear.

Chapter 9

The Way Ahead IS Safe

The years following the Three Mile Island incident in 1979 saw many in the nuclear industry drop their bundle, beaten by the revulsion against radioactivity which, cleverly orchestrated, was taking hold in several communities, particularly among Americans and British. Indeed, the scientists contributed to their own sad condition by stressing the dangers involved. Dick Kovan described the situation well in *New Scientist* (10 December 1988):

> The development of safety philosophy — including concepts such as the Maximum Credible Accident, worst-case analysis and fail-safe technology — may have demonstrated how thorough they were. However they also produced an image of an extremely dangerous technology that was in the hands of a small group of experts and out of the control of the ordinary individual who could only have a sense of impotence in the face of such power.

The result was, in the United States for instance, that more than a hundred nuclear power reactors on order or under construction were cancelled or abandoned. This was due, in part, to earlier over-estimates of total power requirements, and it was a fact that a number of coal-burning power stations were also cancelled. Some incredible situations arose which would have been funny if they were not so wasteful: a power plant was built at Shoreham on Long Island for $5.4 billion but upon completion was not licensed to start generating; the same thing happened to a similar plant at Seabrook in the state of New Hampshire. Additionally, the Department of Energy put out alarming and alarmist reports that it had spent billions of dollars on complex military and civilian energy projects that had simply failed to work as promised; it further reported that all the plants engaged in producing the warhead materials were out of commission, largely due to their age, and would have to be replaced if America's defence plans were to be met. (One suspects that there must have been a goodly number of masochists in the department.) There certainly was, as Dr Ulf Lantzke, director of the International Energy Agency, said: 'A paralysing crisis of confidence in the future of the nuclear industry'. And the anti-nuclear campaigner Amory Lovins who, with his wife, started the Rocky Mountain Institute of Snowmass, Colorado, declared confidently: 'Nuclear energy is dying'.

Well, not really. The phobia never got off the ground in France, the world's most nuclear-powered nation, as the table of nuclear generation shows. From its launch in the 1970s, the French nuclear construction program to reduce dependence on imported coal has never wavered, and by early 1989 it was generating more nuclear power than the country could use, and *Electricité de France* was selling the surplus to every neighboring country — and a further 13,000 megawatts are scheduled to come on stream by the mid-1990s. (When the European Community's Single European Market opens in 1992, wiping out economic frontiers, electricity should flow freely between existing national grids and the French will make heaps.) The Soviet Union, despite Chernobyl, was pursuing 'ambitious expansion of nuclear power plants' to lift production from 9 per cent of all electricity to 15.3 per cent by 1993; Nikolai Ponomarov-Stepnoi, a nuclear scientist, acknowledged to an international

Table of Nuclear Generation

	Percentage of country's power produced by nuclear reactors: **1985** (Source, International Atomic Energy Authority)	**Updates** (Sources, various)
France	59	Going to 75+
Taiwan	52	
Belgium	51	
Finland	41	
Sweden	41	
Switzerland	37	
Bulgaria	29	
West Germany	23	
Japan	23	Now 29, going to 66
Hungary	22	
South Korea	20	
Spain	19	
Britain	17	25 in 1988
United States	14	Now 17.7
Canada	12	
USSR	9	Going to 15.3 now
Average	**29.3**	

Note: Inside the European Community, nuclear power generation has expanded from 5 per cent of the whole in 1973 to more than 25 per cent in 1984 and is projected to account for 40 per cent in 1995.

House of Lords report on Waste Management, London, 1988

conference in Washington that an anti-nuclear movement had sprung up in the Soviet Union; 'this is a new situation for us,' he said. 'Glasnost has opened the floodgates for this movement.' (As if to bear him out, in March 1989 the pride of the Russian merchant fleet, the nuclear-powered monster *Sevmorput*, designed to carry seventy fully-laden barges as its cargo, was denied entry to ports on the Pacific coast after her maiden voyage from Odessa on the Black Sea; after being refused entry at Vladivostok, Nakhodka, Magadan and Vostochny, and being forced to ride out a gale at sea, the city council at Vladivostok, home port for the Soviet Pacific Fleet; relented and let what *Sovietskaya Rossiya* called the 'atomic giant' sail in and berth).

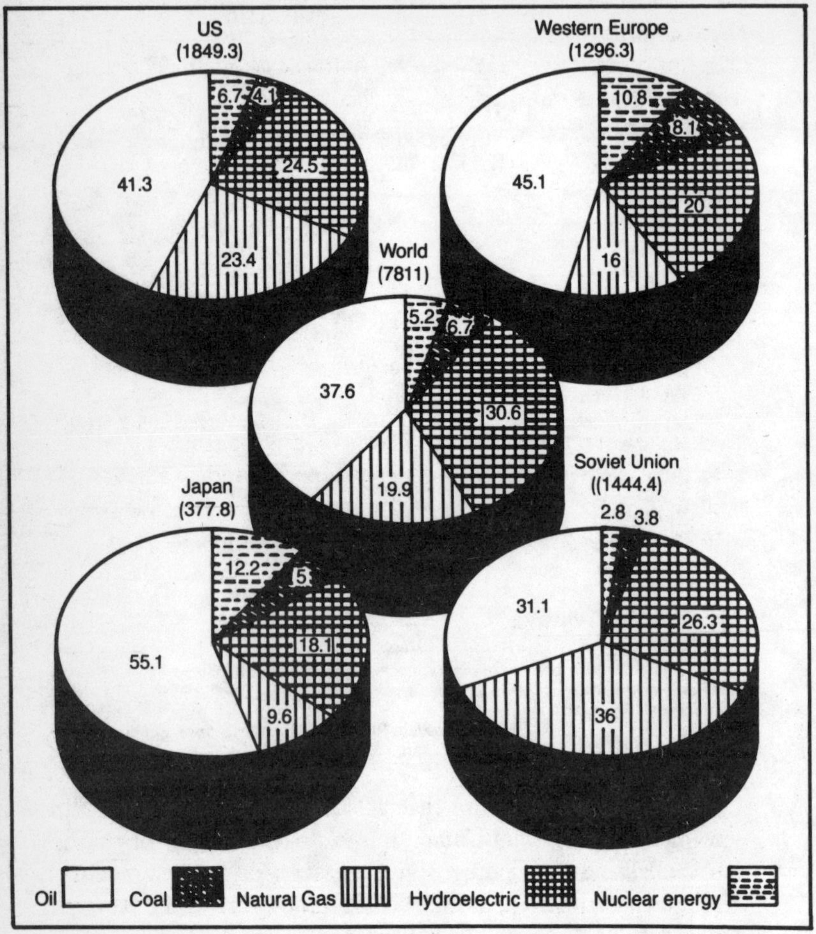

Percentage consumption by fuel in 1987 (million tonnes oil equivalent)

In Japan, too, despite a coalescing of formerly fragmented anti-nuclear groups, the government pressed ahead to lift nuclear power generation from 29.1 per cent of the whole in early 1988 to 66 per cent. (This was good news for Australia; the Kyushu Electric Power Company entered into a contract to take uranium concentrate worth $30 million from the huge Olympic Dam mine, one of the world's biggest deposits of uranium at Roxby Downs in the outback of South Australia, which made its first shipment of yellowcake in 1988.)

In Britain the anti-nuclear ranks had been strong, built on the foundations of CND and fostered by the Friends of the Earth, a daughter group to the founders in America. Indeed, the *New Scientist* said in an editorial:

> So feared is the word 'nuclear' that there are those who baulk at using such harmless phrases as 'nuclear family'. That is why the government has to jump through some remarkable hoops in an attempt to marry two dogmas — its belief in privatisation and its conviction that nuclear power stations are good for the country.

The government's strength resided in Margaret Thatcher who, as we have seen, was one of the first national leaders to realise that concerted efforts had to be made to halt and reverse both the Greenhouse Effect and the Hole in the Sky. But her determination was infectious, a fact picked up by the MP-columnist from Scotland, Tam Dalyell:

> I get the impression that in the aftermath of Chernobyl, many MPs were hauled onto an anti-nuclear bandwagon. I now think they are trying stealthily to clamber down from it. This is partly because they realise that so many livelihoods are at stake, and, to be fair, because they are genuinely concerned about acid rain and the greenhouse effect, which may have more to do with coal-burning stations.

In fact, the British government started selling off its powerhouse, the Central Electricity Generating Board (GEGB) into two privatised companies: National Power, with 70 per cent of the Board's capacity including its nuclear arm, and PowerGen. Announcing details of the sell-off, Energy Minister Cecil Parkinson said that National Power would be provided with a 'cushion' of up to £2.5 billion of taxpayers' money to cope with decommissioning reactors, re-processing spent fuel and disposing of radioactive waste; he added: 'We're not binding the country to nuclear for ever.'

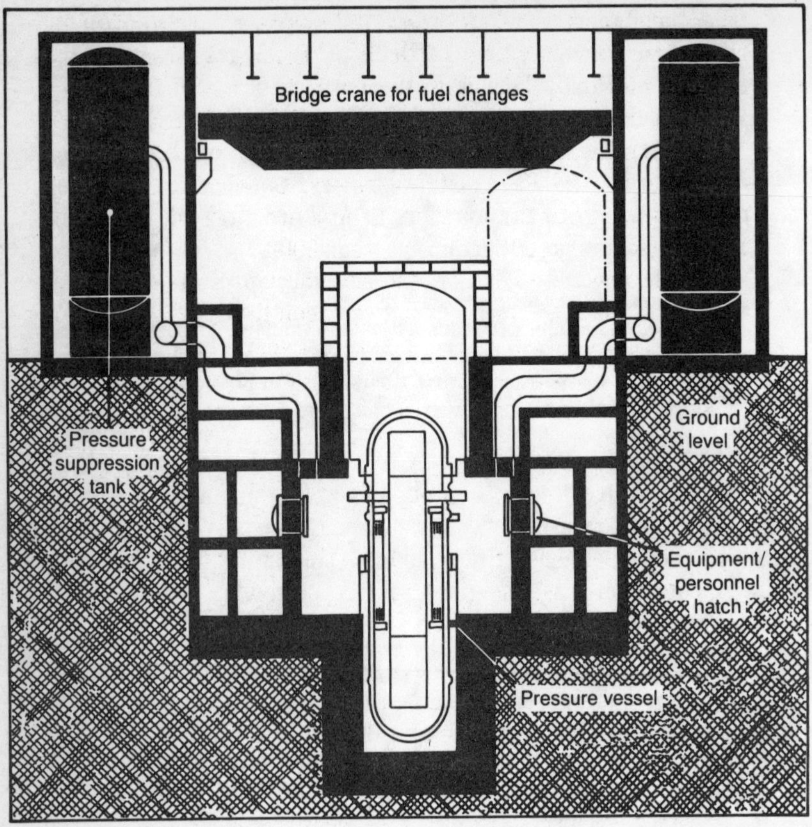

The Safe Integral Reactor takes radioactivity underground

Maybe not. But the government was clearly committed to pursuing reasonable nuclear developments. Its own United Kingdom Atomic Energy Authority (UKAEA) started developing a new concept in power reactors, the mini (300 megawatt) pressurised water reactor which is called Safe Integral Reactor (SIR), whose changed characteristic as far as the lay person is concerned is that the nuclear compartment is underground. Technically, the main change is to a 'passive' safety system in which the emergency cooling water required to prevent a core over-heating is supplied by natural convection instead of by electrically-driven pumps. UKAEA's British associate in the development is Rolls Royce (which has much experience through building the Royal Navy's reactors in nuclear-powered submarines) and together they are working with Cumbustion Engineering and Stone and Websters, two companies which design power plants in America. These are still early days; SIR is aimed at markets beyond the year 2000.

Britain, through UKAEA and also through European agreements, is involved, too, in what has been the great white hope of the nuclear industry since the earliest years: fusion. (Fission, as we know, means splitting; fusion means releasing energy by fusing light atoms together to make heavier ones.) Work has been going on for years: in Britain's case at the Authority's Culham laboratory in Oxfordshire, which is also the home of the Joint European Torus (JET) fusion project; Japan and the United States are also trying, although the wide scientific view is that we will not see fusion until well into the next century. But yet, at the time of writing, interest has been aroused by startling reports from the University of Utah that its Professor of Chemistry, Dr Stanley Pons, and an English electro-chemist, Dr Martin Fleischmann, had created a nuclear fusion reaction in a jam jar at room temperature in their laboratory in Salt Lake City! As the *New Scientist* reported early in April 1989:

> They astounded journalists and annoyed scientists when, two weeks ago, they announced at a press conference that they had achieved "fusion in a test tube" . . . before they had been published in a refereed paper.

They had lowered into a jar filled with heavy water a rod of palladium as a cathode (negative) and a coil of platinum wire as the anode (positive) which were wired to a motor-car battery; when current flowed, positive ions (electrically-charged particles) in the water moved from the anode to the cathode and fused to form helium gas and give off heat. They said that this fairly crude apparatus generated four times as much energy as it consumed, leading *Time* to speculate that this

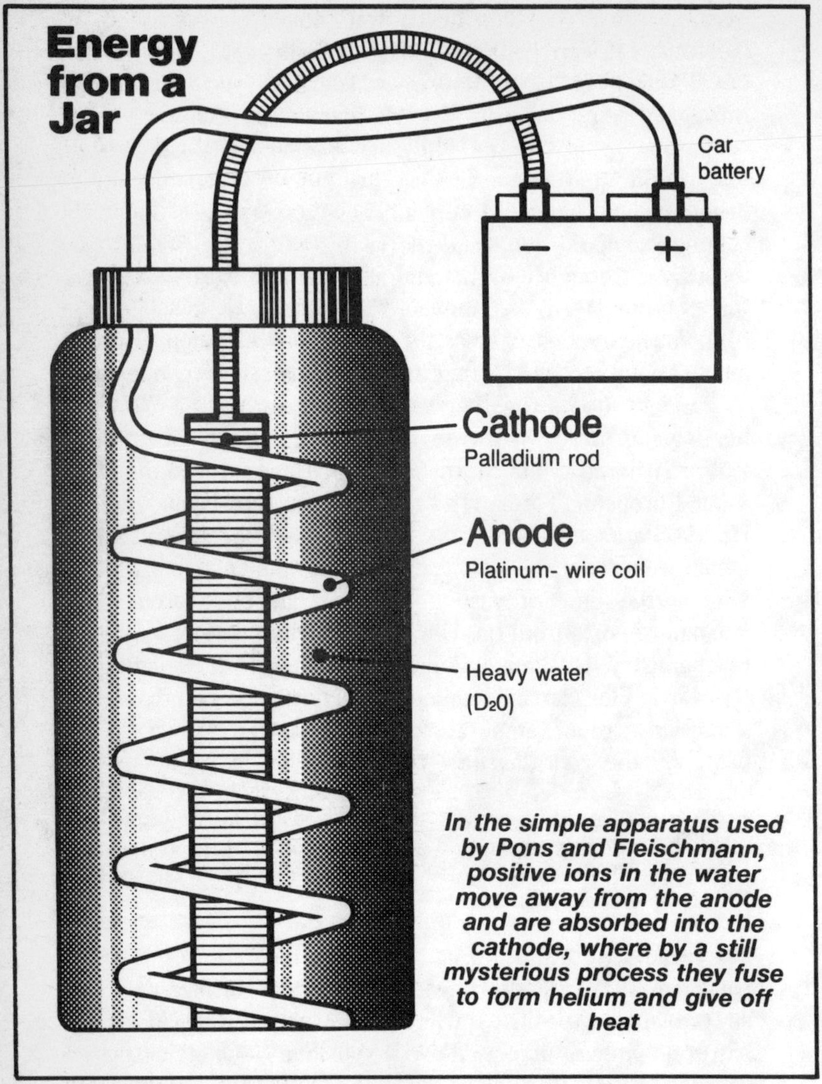

In the simple apparatus used by Pons and Fleischmann, positive ions in the water move away from the anode and are absorbed into the cathode, where by a still mysterious process they fuse to form helium and give off heat

'could conceivably be the biggest science story of the year — if not the decade'.

The scientific community was sceptical — what could a

couple of chemists know about the deepest mystery of nuclear physics? But they were obliged to pay attention when a well-respected physicist at Brigham Young University, Steven Jones, announced that he too had achieved fusion in a jar, but 'with far lower energy output'. Jones said that he had no 'theoretical framework' for this apparent breakthrough in cold fusion, adding: 'We have a Cinderella but no shoe'. Certainly the announcements triggered a flurry of activity in laboratories throughout the world as other researchers sought to replicate the experiments of the ebullient Pons and Fleischmann who, if their work stands up, will be automatic Nobel Prize winners — but it is a big 'if'.

There is confidence that when enough advances are made in fusion technology it will use a heavy isotope of hydrogen called deuterium as the fuel, and thus fulfill the prophesy by Jules Verne in *The Mysterious Island* that 'water may be the coal of the future', for deuterium is obtained from water! There is further confidence that fusion is 'virtually inexhaustible', which led John Elkington to write in his book *Sun Traps* that 'there is every prospect that its (fusion's) contribution to global energy supplies could vastly exceed that available from all the other renewable-energy resources put together'.

Perhaps one of the more interesting later developments has been in the United States. In what the *New York Times* described as 'the opening salvo in a battle to return the U.S. nuclear power industry to the robust good health it enjoyed before being halted in its tracks by a public outcry following a partial meltdown at Three Mile Island', President Ronald Reagan, in the closing months of his second term, signed a crucial order. On the face of it the four-page executive order seemed rather obscure; it gave the Federal Emergency Management Agency the power to draft evacuation plans for nuclear power stations whenever state or local governments 'decline or fail to prepare plans of their own'. It was through the device of failing to draw up evacuation plans that the multi-billion nuclear power stations at Shoreham and Seabrook, mentioned earlier, had been turned into white elephants; a White House official acknowledged that Reagan's order was designed to break the deadlock.

Next came the significant step that Governor John Sununu of New Hampshire, who had fought long, strenuously and almost alone for the Seabrook power station in his state to be put into commission, was appointed Chief of Staff by Reagan's successor and the present President, George Bush. Soon after Bush was sworn in, the AP-Dow Jones financial news service put out a story from Washington which said, in part:

> Mr Bush is laying the groundwork for a nationwide revival of nuclear power, and he seems to have enough support in Congress to carry out his aims. The new administration wants . . . to make it possible to build and operate a commercial plant in three or four years instead of the current ten to fifteen years now required. It also wants to encourage consortia to design and build better reactors, even if foreign partners are required.

As if in answer to a prayer, a group of companies led by General Atomic Corporation of San Diego, California, announced the development of a new type of modular reactor which is safer than conventional reactors. The key safety feature is that the uranium fuel is in tiny particles, the size of a grain of sand, each encapsulated in multiple spheres of glassy carbon-based materials which trap radioactive fission products and can transmit heat but remain intact up to temperatures of 1,815 degrees Celsius — some 200 degrees hotter than the fuel grains can achieve. The *New York Times* reported that its 'designers say the machine is intrinsically safe because its physical characteristics make it immune to meltdown, the most feared reactor accident'. Additionally, the inert gas helium is used as the coolant and, for further safety, the core size and reactor output is limited to about 140 megawatts, hence the modular aspect — several can operate in tandem to produce greater quantities of power. General Atomic said that Seimens of West Germany and a Swedish–Swiss joint venture of Asea Brown Boveri were combining to market the concept in Europe and are also helping the Soviet Union to build one, and in Japan Toshiba and IHI Heavy Industries are investigating the design.

This safer concept plus the underground Safe Integral Reactor (SIR) point to a new generation of reactors for power plants which are more reassuring. They are doubly welcome because they are so urgently required to cope with environment problems. Lando Zech, the head of the Nuclear Regulatory Commission which issues licences for reactors to operate in America, said at the end of 1988 that 'nuclear power plants have become safer and more efficient over the last four years', adding: 'The future hinges on a demonstrated record of plant safety . . . An accident at a plant anywhere in the world will have adverse international repercussions.'

Oh, and there's still the ongoing problem of waste!

Part

3

Waste Not Want Not

Chapter 10

One for the Too-Hard Basket

Nuclear waste has been a problem. While most nuclear scientists pretended it did not exist, most lay people saw it as perhaps the biggest barrier to the onward use of nuclear power. The European Commission, the bureaucrats of the European Community, conducted a series of four public opinion polls from 1982 to 1987 in which they asked the twelve thousand people interviewed to rank in order the risks, as they saw them, of nuclear power; Monsieur J. C. Charrault, head of the division for nuclear policy, reported in 1988 that in all four surveys 'waste disposal was always at the top of the perceived risks. The risk of effluent releases during normal plant operation was second. The third was the explosion of a nuclear plant, like an atomic bomb.'

In the United States, attitudes about nuclear waste have switched over the years. Way back in 1960, *Nuclear News* reported that a poll concerning a reactor at Indian Point showed that 57 per cent of people 'felt confident that waste isolation was safe'. By 1974 a survey by Opinion Research Corporation showed that 52 per cent of people 'believed that waste management was a serious problem'. And since 1978 Harris polls have shown regularly that while a majority of Americans continued to support nuclear power, majorities of two-to-one have been opposed to nuclear plants within five miles of their own homes — the birth of the Nimby Syndrome: Not In My Back Yard. Not surprisingly, the fall in enthusiasm for nuclear power was either the result of or the cause for anti-nuclear groups and organisations like Friends of the Earth and Greenpeace becoming influential. Therefore, there is particular interest in a U.S.-wide survey conducted by Robert Cameron Mitchell in 1978 for his paper 'The Public Speaks Again: A New Environmental Survey' published in *Resources*. Mitchell asked people about their attitude to the anti-nuclear movement, getting them to say if they were active participants, sympathetic to the movement, neutral, unsympathetic or simply did not know. Result:

Active participant	2%
Sympathetic	27%
Neutral	44%
Unsympathetic	21%
Don't know	6%

For every person who was an active supporter or sympathiser with the anti-nuclearists, there were more than two who were either opposed or not involved. And such support as they had was not always voluntary — as the following dialogue between Baroness White and Stewart Boyle, 'national energy organiser' for Friends of the Earth in Britain, before the House of Lords select committee on radioactive waste management testifies:

> *Baroness White*: It so happens that in 1981 I lived on the edge of Merioneth [where geological investigation of a possible waste disposal site was frustrated] and I saw exactly what happened there in stirring up public opinion. It was the most unscientific and the most emotional incident that in a fairly long public life I have witnessed. The organisation there was to frighten people. It was organised very skilfully so as to prevent any geologist going on any farmer's land even to begin prospecting for where one might conceivably drill. Farmers there could have been frightened that their person, their family or their stock might have been under some form of attack. They called this outfit Madryn — the Welsh

for fox — and thoroughly organised it. I have seen the way in which public opinion, on an entirely non-scientific emotional basis, can be manipulated, and I am concerned. You complain about our not knowing; but persons — I do not say your own organisation directly; but very closely compatible ones — do their best to make sure that one does not know.
Boyle: Perhaps I can answer that. First, I must rebut some of the things that you have just said about the Welsh campaign.
White: Were you part of it?
Boyle: No, I was not part of it. But any suggestion that pressure was put on local farmers to go along with the anti-dumping of waste, otherwise their sheep would be rustled or burned, I am afraid is complete news to me, and it is not something which I personally . . .
White: It is not news to me, and I lived there.

Waste comes at the back end of the nuclear cycle. The cycle starts with the mining of uranium ore. Notable deposits are in Canada's north-west territories, specifically beside Great Bear Lake whose main settlement is Port Radium; Zaire, formerly the Belgian Congo; Gabon, Namibia and Australia (where the government disreputably has an each-way bet, allowing three deposits to be worked for considerable export earnings but not permitting other known sources to be developed; hypocrisy and humbug). On site the ore is ground to a fine powder and treated to extract yellow cake (U_3O_8). More than 100,000 tonnes of ore are required to produce the 180 tonnes of yellow cake needed to yield enough fuel to run a 1,000-megawatt nuclear power station for a year. The yellow cake is transported to an enrichment plant where the percentage of fissile Uranium-235 is lifted from 0.7 per cent to 3.0 per cent and fuel rods are made. During fission in the power station, about 10 tonnes of fuel (or up to 30 tonnes in some American plants) are spent in a year and have to be replaced; the spent ones become waste and go into temporary storage under water. Wastes are produced at every stage and are divided into two categories: low-level waste (LLW) and high-level waste (HLW). Low-level waste must be isolated for between 100 and 1,000 years while it becomes innocuous; and high-level waste must be stored for very much longer because it remains radioactive for certainly 100,000 years and perhaps 1 million years or longer. It is, naturally, the high-level waste which causes particular consternation.

It is the spent fuel rods which generate high-level waste. In some nuclear countries, when rods are taken from temporary under-water storage they are moved to re-processing plants where re-usable uranium is recovered and plutonium isolated out; this leaves the ultimate waste and it amounts to only 4.1 per cent of the spent rods — from the original 10 tonnes, only 410 kilograms have to be coped with, not a big job from the quantity point of view, although they contain most of the radioactivity. At the time of writing only four countries had re-processing plants in action: France, Britain, West Germany and Japan.

There is no doubt that waste disposal was rough in the early days — not least, probably, because atomic and hydrogen bombs were being tested in the atmosphere right through the 1950s and into the 1960s by the United States, Britain, the Soviet Union and France and the whole of the earth's atmosphere was being radioactively polluted over and over again. What added harm could a bit of waste from a nuclear reactor do?

The first handlers of waste were, of course, the bomb-makers who worked under the protection of complete secrecy. That fine reporter, Ed Magnuson, looked backward in *Time* (31 October 1988):

> The private contractors who ran the major U.S. weapons plants released huge quantities of radioactive particles into the air and dumped tons of potentially cancer-inducing refuse into flowing creeks and leaking pits, contaminating underground water supplies in a seepage that cannot be stopped . . . and no one in relevant offices seemed to care. Why? Because a legalistic, bureaucratic shuffle left no one responsible for whatever human and environmental damage was inflicted.

British engineers were clearly being just as cavalier, pumping waste from their first re-processing plant at Windscale into the Irish Sea which, in time, became nicknamed by one newspaper 'the Plutonium Sea'. Shielded by secrecy laws and almost-total public ignorance, the dumping might have gone on and on. But the right phrase at the right time can alert a sleeping people; such a phrase was coined in the tabloid *Daily Mirror* on 21 October 1975 when it described Britain as 'the world's nuclear dustbin'. This referred to an application by British Nuclear Fuels Limited (BNF — a wholly-owned subsidiary of the Atomic Energy Authority) to build a new plant at Windscale to re-process fuel from home and abroad — specifically Japanese nuclear waste under a contract worth 'hundreds of millions of pounds' according to Tony Hall in *Nuclear Politics*; that phrase — 'world's nuclear dustbin' — did 'above all set the nuclear debate alight'. The responsible Minister at the time, the left-wing Tony Benn, told the House of Commons:

> The only way the Government can respond to anxieties is by adopting policies of the greatest possible openness, disclosing and publicising all the information that Parliament or the people wish to have.

A Royal Commission on Environmental Pollution, which was sitting at the time of the dustbin disclosure under the chairmanship of Sir Brian Flowers, was quite clear about waste when it reported in 1976:

> We are agreed that it would be irresponsible and morally wrong to commit future generations to the consequences of fission power on a massive scale unless it has been demonstrated beyond reasonable doubt that at least one method exists for the safe isolation of these wastes for the indefinite future.

No such method did *then* exist.

No nation has shown a greater commitment to nuclear power than the French (who continue atomic testing on Mururoa Atoll in the South Pacific, much to the fury of Australia, New Zealand and the islanders of the region). They started re-processing at Marcoule, by the River Rhone, more than thirty years ago and today the *Compagnie Générale des Matières Nucléaires* (COGEMA — a wholly-owned subsidiary of the French Atomic

Energy Commission) operates two re-processing plants at *Cap de la Hague*, about 12 miles (20 kilometres) from Cherbourg, a port on the English Channel; the establishment has a near-surface storage nearby at *Centre de la Manche*. The French pioneered the borosilicate-glass method of solidifying high-level waste. (Borosilicate — salts containing the non-metallic solid element boron — *Concise Oxford*) This is what it involves: the high-level waste coming from re-processing plants is in a nitric acid solution and must be converted into a solid, long-lasting form. So the solution is fed into a furnace to evaporate off the nitric acid. The remaining waste particles are mixed with the glass-forming materials and the whole is melted down. The resulting glass is poured into steel cylinders to solidify, the cylinders being sealed later by remote-control techniques. The fission-product wastes — strontium 90 and caesium 137 — which make up between 10 and 20 per cent of the glass continue to give off great heat, so the cylinders have to be stored in air-cooled vaults. (The stores have a series of vertical holes in a strong concrete base into which the waste cylinders are lowered; cool air is circulated round the cylinders.) The risk is that if the centre of the glass blocks in the cylinders are allowed to go to a temperature of 700 degrees centigrade (and in some cases much lower temperatures) the glass might deteriorate — that is the crucial problem with borosilicate glass; but for years it was considered the best wasteform despite serious shortcomings. Even so, neither the French nor anyone else, have gone any further than storing the glass waste cylinders in temporary vaults; no one has yet been game to commit the cylinders to a final resting place.

While the British as well as the Germans (at Karlsruhe and at Wackersdorf), the Belgians (at Mol) and the Japanese (at Tokai Mura) have followed France down the re-processing and vitrification (glass) route, they have all struck strife in their searches for geological burial grounds. In the late 1970s, Britain's Energy Minister Michael Heseltine announced that fifteen sites in suitable igneous rock — stretching from Gwynedd in Wales through the English midlands and the Scottish highlands to the Western Isles — would be tested in the hope of finding two or three which met the specifications. The job was never completed; as soon as permission was sought to drill test holes the local inhabitants organised successful protests. Then, in 1983, it was arbitrarily announced that dumps would be established at Elstow in Bedfordshire and Billingham in County Durham; but these, too, had to be abandoned in the face of public fury locally. The problem has still not been resolved — despite suggestions by Dr Lewis Roberts, director of the Harwell research establishment, that communities should be bribed with jobs, improved facilities and money to accept a dump in their back yard. Early in 1989 Virginia Bottomley, the junior Environment Minister, admitted in Parliament that Britain had more than half a million litres of high-level waste awaiting permanent disposal! In West Germany, legal actions by the anti-nuclear lobby have halted the transportation of waste to a new dump at Ahaus, near the Dutch border. (Back in 1979, West Germany did a deal with the late President Sadat to ship waste to Egypt for disposal, but opposition from environmentalists was too strong and the project was abandoned.)

All nuclear nations have had their protests, and in Japan the world's fourth largest nuclear industry was shocked when 20,000 people-plus demonstrated in Tokyo on the second anniversary of Chernobyl; and, as Michael Cross reported in *New Scientist* early in 1989, the decision to locate a high-level waste store at Horonobe, in the northern island of Hokkaido, 'is likely to cause more protests'. (Currently, Japan sends some of its spent fuel to Britain and France for re-processing and then takes the final waste back for temporary near-surface storage.)

Arguably, the United States has got itself into the worst waste mess of all as the nuclear industry suffers a meltdown in public support. Its dilemma involves not only high-level waste disposal but low-level as well. At a cost of $700 million and over five years, a massive cavern to take long-held waste from America's nuclear weapons plants was gouged out of deep salt formations beneath the desert near Carlsbad, New Mexico, just 30 miles (48 kilometres) north of the Mexican border. It was due to be opened in October 1988, but just a month beforehand that was 'postponed indefinitely', according to the *New York Times*, which went on:

> The Waste Isolation Pilot Plant is an enormous grid of mile-long corridors, huge storage rooms and deep ventilation shafts mined 2,150 feet (650 metres) under the desert. It is designed to store millions of cubic feet of radioactive wastes from 45 years of atomic weapon production . . . Leaks have appeared in the vast underground cavern, which was designed to be bone dry forever.

The crisis was compounded immediately when Cecil Andrus, Governor of the state of Idaho and a former Secretary of the Interior, ordered his state police to stop any more shipments of military waste coming in from over its borders. This was serious because at the Idaho National Engineering Laboratory some 120,000 drums and 11,000 boxes of military waste were already in 'temporary' storage pending the opening of the cavern in New Mexico!

The situation for high-level waste remains similarly depressing, as *Fortune* reported in late 1987:

> While twenty-five states vie to be the home of the U.S. supercollider — the huge nuclear accelerator for studying sub-atomic particles — the Department of Energy can find no host for the first long-term repository for high-level nuclear waste. After five years and $1.1 billion, the DOE has not come up with a state that will allow detailed preliminary under-ground research.

As happened in Britain, bribery was discussed; among a flurry of bills on the subject to be introduced to the Congress was one which proposed the payment of $50 million a year to any state 'or Indian tribal reservation' which would allow site testing and a further $100 million a year if the testing led to an actual dump.

Nowhere was real progress being made and frustration abounded. No one felt it more than Gathorne Gathorne-Hardy, the fifth Earl of Cranbrook and a man of scientific background who had done zoology with the great Solly Zuckerman; he chaired, through 1987–8, the House of Lords select committee looking into radioactive waste management, whose report was circulated in October 1988. It was quite definite:

> The committee is convinced that permanent disposal for all categories of wastes is an acceptable solution to the environmental problems posed by radioactive wastes. It believes that decisions should not be deferred to future generations . . . The committee recommends that deep geological disposal for high-level and long-lived wastes should be pursued with determination. *No better solution is discernable and it is irresponsible to wait any longer for some hoped-for but unspecified alternative.*

I have added the italics because, throughout the report's 264 pages covering written evidence from seventeen interested bodies and verbal question-and-answer sessions with thirty-three witnesses, there is no reference whatsoever to a discovery which can solve the problem, not just for the British but for all the nuclear nations. A discovery that was already ten years old!

Chapter

11

The Earthly Professor's Solution

As a young fellow Alfred Edward Ringwood had no dreams of becoming an engine driver when he grew up; instead, he planned to become a gold prospector and thus make his fortune. As a cheerily-confident scholarship boy at Geelong Grammar — a boarding academy some forty miles from Melbourne for sons of the wealthier Australian establishment — he would ride his bicycle eighteen miles to the abandoned mining township of Steiglitz to fossick for gold, quite successfully. His first degree at the University of Melbourne, again on a scholarship, was bachelor of science in geology and he stayed on to complete his master's and then his doctor of philosophy — PhDs were a new vogue in the early 1950s and his was only the second in the geology department and among the first dozen from the whole university.

As an economic geologist and geophysicist he got heavily into applied research, developing with a colleague a process for extracting rutile (titanium dioxide) and white-paint pigment from beach sands, which earned him rights of £3,000 (*$50,000 in 1989 values*). As an academic, Ted Ringwood has always been a practical man; while geologically mapping the Snowy Mountains during his university days he visited an old silver mine and observed that they had thrown away all the galena (lead sulphide, the commonest ore of lead) as waste, so he organised friends and a pack horse to get the stuff out and sold it to the historic shot tower in Melbourne, which is today enshrined in the Victoria Central development. It too made him useful money.

It was during eighteen months as a post-doctoral researcher at Harvard University in America that Ringwood met John Jaeger, the Head of the Department of Geophysics in the Research School of Physical Sciences at the Australian National University in Canberra. ANU was opened soon after World War Two specifically as a graduate research university, designed to reverse the brain-drain of clever Australians to places of learning overseas; Jaeger succeeded with Ringwood, who joined the geophysics department at the beginning of 1959.

Ringwood has stayed at ANU for more than thirty years and has had a remarkable career in earth sciences; he has published more than three hundred academic papers, a prodigious output of learning, as well as books including *Composition and Petrology of the Earth's Mantle* and *Origin of the Earth and Moon.* While almost unknown to the lay public, Ringwood has been widely recognised by his peers: Fellow of the Royal Society, Member of the Australian Academy of Science, foreign associate of the National Academy of Sciences of the United States and he has received awards and medals from scientific societies in Britain, America, Russia, Germany and Canada as well as Australia.

Ringwood's path at ANU saw him appointed Professor of Geophysics in 1963 at the age of thirty-three, Professor of Geochemistry in 1967 and for six years (1978-84) Director of the Research School of Earth Sciences which had been spun off from the School of Physical Sciences. He married soon after settling in Canberra and raised two children there. And, while most of his published material was the result of fundamental research, he has made two excursions into practical research, one concerning nuclear waste and the other the development of a whole new generation of diamond-cutting tools.

His interest in nuclear waste was triggered in the 1970s by Sir Edward Bullard, the distinguished Cambridge scientist who, by accurately mapping the beds of oceans, revealed the role of tectonic plates in the making of earthquakes, and who later advised governments on the detection of underground nuclear explosions. Bullard was an old man and dying of cancer when he last visited Australia but he aroused Ringwood's interest when he made the point — since published by Ringwood — that 'the disciplines most directly concerned with understanding the behaviour of High Level Waste when buried in the earth are the geological sciences. Surprisingly enough, this obvious fact has been widely neglected in the past.' But it was not this truth which stirred Ringwood into action. At the time, late 1976, some people were speculating that the best answer might be to shoot the waste into outer space, a proposition which alarmed Ringwood. He resolved: 'I'm going to do something about it.'

For the next eighteen months he and his team — Dr Sue Kesson, Nick Ware, Bill Hibberson and Alan Major — worked on the problem. Ringwood habitually wakened at three or four o'clock in the morning for concentrated thinking sessions during which he planned his team's next step: 'I proceeded by conceptual leaps and intuitive bounds. At first I was encouraged, then optimistic and finally convinced. One knew one had a system.'

The starting point, naturally, was the earth itself . . .

> Many natural minerals are known to have the capacity to accept radioactive waste elements into their crystal lattices and to retain these elements very tightly. A number of minerals within this category are *known* to have been stable in a wide range of geological and geochemical environments for periods ranging from 20 million to 2,000 million years. By comparison, the *maximum* period which is needed for decay of radioactive elements in reactor wastes is less then 1 million years. Thus, these natural minerals have demonstrated their capacity to retain safely dangerous radioactive waste elements for periods sufficient to ensure their decay.

If one could replicate such ancient rocks and minerals and use them to immobilise High Level Waste the result would surely be safer than the glass then being used and known to be of limited reliability.

Ringwood announced the result at a press conference on Thursday 27 July 1978: Synroc — synthetic rock. Unusually, the work was described in a sixty-page book, *Safe Disposal of High Level Nuclear Reactor Wastes: A New Strategy* by A. E. Ringwood, which was released simultaneously in Britain, the United States and Australia, instead of appearing first in an academic journal — a decision prompted by the ANU publicity people which Ringwood now regrets, although the publicity was massive; front-page news throughout the world in all languages.

> Although the individual minerals are very refractory [resistant], our investigations have shown that a mixture of these minerals . . . can be converted into a synthetic rock of well-formed crystals . . . The resulting Synroc mixture is then melted and allowed to crystallise. During crystallisation, the radioactive waste elements enter the lattices of the minerals of the synthetic rock to form highly stable, dilute solid solutions.

All fields of scientific research are somewhat crowded on a global perspective, therefore it is quite unusual to get a clean break — to announce a discovery such as Synroc without someone else claiming to have got there first. Professor Rustum Roy, Director of the Materials Research Laboratory at Pennsylvania State University, was the one to cry foul: 'Professor Ringwood has confirmed in virtually identical words what we have been saying for at least four or five years . . . But what he said on how you make it is nonsense from an engineering point of view . . . The process he has come up with is not a particularly good one. We rejected it at least four years ago.' Ringwood responded immediately: 'Our solution — the composition of the synthetic rock I have called Synroc — does not remotely resemble anything ever proposed by Penn State.' Ten years later he can say: 'Roy and his team went off in the wrong direction. What they produced was not good enough!' Crucially, and contrary to Roy's forecast, Synroc was quite quickly granted a patent in the United States, as it was everywhere else where an application was made, confirming that it was indeed a totally new concept.

The brush with Roy induced Ringwood to announce for the first time the chemical composition by weight of Synroc: titania 57 per cent, barium oxide 4, alumina 4, zirconia 6 and lime 9 — they are all widely available — with the high-level waste filling the remaining 20 per cent.

To complete the operation, Ringwood proposed that the waste-bearing Synroc should be pressed — in specially-designed, concertina-like metal canisters which, when squashed into large round pellets, look like an enlarged discus — and then buried in deep drill holes into rock, the deepest being about three kilometres below the surface (some mines are much deeper and the drilling techniques are well established) and the shallowest two kilometres down, the top of the holes being plugged with clay.

Within a year Synroc was under investigation throughout the nuclear world, $2 million being spent in half a dozen American laboratories alone. And at the jubilee conference of ANZAAS (Australian and New Zealand Association for the Advancement of Science) in July 1980, Ringwood outlined a total scheme which he claimed — and the *New Scientist* agreed — would be vital to nuclear non-proliferation. It would have put Australia at the centre of the cycle. Ringwood proposed that Australia build a plant to enrich the uranium which had been discovered in its ground and to make fuel rods; the rods would then be *leased* to the countries which wanted them and *returned* after use for re-processing and for the wastes to be incorporated in Synroc and buried. Such a scheme, he said, would 'eliminate the possibility that Australian uranium might be used by foreign countries to produce nuclear weapons and would also result in the establishment of major new industries of immense economic benefit to the nation.'

Scientists throughout the world were much interested in Synroc but few firm moves were made towards its adoption; glass was in place as the most-accepted waste receptacle. But a vital test came in the late 1970s when the United States government decided to build and operate a Defence Waste Processing Facility (DWPF) at the huge Savannah River nuclear war plant near Aiken, South Carolina, which had been making waste for more than twenty years and was storing *millions of gallons* of it in underground tanks! Seventeen candidate waste forms were originally reviewed; they included Synroc D, a variant on the original because of the different composition of defence waste compared with power-station waste. The seventeen were quickly reduced to seven and then, after two years work at Savannah River, to two: Synroc and borosilicate glass.

The United States Department of Energy's final *Evaluation and Selection of Candidate High-Level Waste Forms* did come down on the side of glass. (The contractor running the Savannah River plant was E. I. du Pont de Nemours & Co, of CFC and other fame, who just happened to have the American manufacturing rights for borosilicate glass! Ringwood says: 'That was 99 per cent of the decision.') The official basis for the choice was that glass was preferred because 'process complexity, development requirements and programmatic costs' (whatever those gobbledegook terms might mean) 'were determined to be less' for glass than Synroc. But the report did concede that 'Synroc D would be a suitable waste form for long-term isolation of Savannah River Plant waste. No phenomena have been observed that would significantly degrade the ceramics's ability to limit radionuclide release from a repository.' A strong vote of confidence.

Indeed, it was agreed that the Department of Energy would run a $16 million research and development program over three years using both glass and Synroc to find out which one really was best. But at the crucial moment President Jimmy Carter was slung out of the White House after only one term to be replaced by Ronald Reagan; the program was axed. 'We came within a whisker of scoring a major hit,' Ringwood recalls ruefully. A practical advance was made when the Australian Atomic Energy Commission (now the Australian Nuclear Science and Technology Organisation — ANSTO) and Ringwood's ANU team started a collaboration to design and build a nonradioactive demonstration Synroc plant at the Commission's headquarters at Lucas Heights on Sydney's southern outskirts; this was eventually to have a capital cost of some $4 million. The work, as *New Scientist* explained, involved . . .

> Mixing, heating and pressing chemicals that are easily available. These are calcium carbonate, barium carbonate, zirconium oxide, aluminium oxide and a form of titanium dioxide. When properly prepared and given the right heat and pressure treatments, the mixture is converted into a combination of only three minerals. The result is a dense black rock that is so hard that diamond-impregnated tools have to be used to machine it. Remarkably, the three constituent minerals between them incorporate the entire range of about twenty elements found in high-level wastes, with the result that they become an integral part of the crystal structure of the minerals that form Synroc.

The thing which Synroc had to do was prove beyond doubt that it was superior to glass as a long-term wasteform and the key element was the ability to resist leaching by water deep underground. Tests were done, in addition to ANU and ANSTO, at the Lawrence Livermore Laboratories and the Battelle Pacific Northwest Laboratories in the United States and at the Institute for Chemical Technology at Julich in West Germany, using both real and simulated nuclear wastes. (Ongoing tests are being done under inter-government agreements between Australia, Britain, France and Japan.) A fair summary of results shows that the long-term leach rates of the dangerous elements caesium and strontium from Synroc are *a thousand times less* than glass and — bearing in mind that leach rates increase with rising temperatures — the long-term rates for Synroc are again about a thousand less than those of glass at 95 degrees centigrade and *about ten thousand less* at 200 degrees centigrade. Convincing stuff.

But the nuclear world was not ready to be convinced. The French had jumped into glass twenty years earlier, building a plant at Marcoule; it now enjoys a dominance, taking in spent fuel from such countries as Japan, Germany, Sweden, Belgium, Switzerland and the Netherlands for re-processing, returning the waste solidified as glass. As the United States Department of Energy has reported, 'the fact that France has a licensed and successfully-operating vitrification (glass) process weighs heavily on the selection of initial immobilization facilities'. The key word is 'initial'. Glass, because of its vulnerability to leaching and other factors, decays over quite a short time-span. It is only a short-term answer. Synroc is the long-term solution. But, despite Ted Ringwood's best efforts at educating and selling, the head-in-the-sand approach held sway.

Chapter 12

Synroc Finds a Friend

Timothy Paul Hopwood might well be the man the nuclear industry in general and Synroc in particular so urgently need. He is an entrepreneur with a wide background in earth sciences; he understands the problem and how to solve it. He also personifies the characteristics so often wrongly attributed to Australians who, for the most part, are urban sybarites who prefer to be spectators rather than players. Descended from a convict — Henry Hopwood was transported from Lancashire for receiving stolen silk and, after serving his time in Tasmania, established the important border town of Echuca by operating a ferry across the Murray River — our Hopwood has a well-developed spirit of enquiring adventure and a proper disregard for most bureaucrats and academic pomposity.

Tim Hopwood's father grew vegetables for a living in the Gosford district north of Sydney, an area where a boy could observe layers of rock in cliffs and headlands every day. This interest was heightened by a grandfather who was a coal miner on the Newcastle field a little further north. Grandfather Hopwood took Tim underground in the Redhead mine when he was seven, and when he was twelve bought him a copy of the first edition of *Geology of Australia* by Edgeworth David, the distinguished Professor of Geology at the University of Sydney. Two scholarships moved Hopwood from Gosford High School into the science faculty of that university where he read geology, physics, chemistry and mathematics in first year, but concentrated more and more on geology, getting first-class honours in his BSc degree. This success suggested further study and research; a crack at his PhD. His field was structural geology, the nature of the earth's crust. To finance his research, Hopwood lectured at the university and spent four summers in Tasmania mapping for the Aberfoyle Tin Partnership NL (now simply Aberfoyle) and this was a success, too: 'I mapped Mount Cleveland in north-western Tasmania; we were lucky and scored. I was able to see what happens to a project from the grass-roots stage, through drilling (luckily my structure worked out) and into production; the Cleveland Tin Mine has been a good little producer for twenty-five years, it gave Aberfoyle its start.' Few geologists have such satisfaction; Hopwood speculates: 'Discoveries which lead to a mine are made by about one geologist in twenty-five in his entire lifetime. Of the three hundred geology graduates in Australia this year, very few will ever find a viable mine.' Five years after starting out, Hopwood's thesis on *Structural Style and Metamorphic Grades in the Cooma Complex of New South Wales* secured him his doctorate and he looked forward to a career as an academic.

But minerals were on the move. The same year Hopwood got his PhD, Western Mining Corporation, under the urging of its Kalgoorlie manager Arvi Parbo, started sinking a shaft at what is now Kambalda to become the world's fourth-largest nickel producer. That year, too, BHP in partnership with Esso struck oil in Bass Strait. And in 1968 the nonferrous metals share index zoomed from 2216.58 to 3692.49 on the Sydney Stock Exchange, a rise of better than 66 per cent. Suddenly geologists were in demand. Excitement grew into a mania when, on 25 September 1969, an obscure exploration company based in Adelaide, Poseidon NL, jumped 33 cents to close at

$1.48 on brisk trading, triggering what Trevor Sykes has described as 'the wildest phenomenon ever recorded on Australian stock exchanges'. It lasted five months and Poseidon shares peaked at an incredible $280.00 a share. Early in the boom Hopwood quietly formalised his consulting work through a private company, having done field work for Utah Development at Mount Morgan in Queensland and Girilambone in New South Wales, where he located copper — some 4 million tonnes at 2.2 per cent — 'not a bad little deposit'.

A lecturing post at the University of Adelaide, teaching structural geology and optics-for-mineralogy, won Hopwood back to academia, temporarily — at a salary drop from about $10,500 a year to $6,500; but soon lost him again to Mining Finance Corporation, an off-shoot of the aggressive British entrepreneurs Slater Walker, at a tempting $20,000, which was a top salary twenty years ago. When the boom turned to bust, so did Mining Finance Corporation; but Hopwood was hooked into consulting (returning to teaching only for short stints at the University of Melbourne in 1974 and as Millercom Visiting Professor of Geology at the University of Illinois in 1979); indeed, because geological investigations can only be carried out on the spot, he became something of a world wanderer, accompanied always by his wife Margaret (Meg), another scholarship student at the University of Sydney who, although her main subject had been geography, had done enough geology to be a most useful assistant. A passion for travel made a nomadic married life desirable until they felt it was time to have children.

Their first assignment was at the Redbank copper find in the Northern Territory of Australia. 'We scored there, too, finding another two million tonnes to put with the two they had already.' Then across to the Nabarlek uranium deposit near the Oenpelli mission station in Arnhem Land; Hopwood's job, with Colin Brooks and Bert Mason, was to re-calculate the size of the deposit which was estimated originally at 55,000 tonnes. They measured only 11,000 tonnes, which caused considerable fuss; in the event Nabarlek yielded 12,500 tonnes — 'So we were pretty right'. Hopwood recalls that Nabarlek introduced him to the politics of uranium and gave him useful background.

A friend who was working in America asked Hopwood if he would go to Morocco, in north-western Africa, to work on the belief that, as a result of continental drift many millions of years ago, Morocco complemented the geology of the south-eastern United States; the assignment was to make on-site observations in the High Atlas Mountains and work out from them the structural sections. Hopwood said to Meg: 'Look, we've got no kids. So let's jump on a plane and give it a go.' He bought two one-way tickets from Adelaide to Rabat and they spent the next three months tripping back and forth in a small four-wheel-drive Renault — 'a bit like a pram' — and pitching their tent on a new camp site each night. They lived on the food they bought in local markets and Meg recalls: 'The meat that was killed that day you ate that day, because there was no refrigeration; we had to boil it and boil it to make it tender enough to eat'. For a decent meal, and a shower or bath, they repaired to cities like Fez or Marrakesh every three or four days.

A complete change of locale in the northern summer of 1972 came with a shift to the lakes and fir forests of northern Ontario, not far south of Hudson's Bay, to identify targets for copper and zinc investigations. Hopwood recalls: 'Canadians have bear stories like Australians have snake stories. A bear did destroy one of our camps; they're a nuisance rather than a problem . . . I don't have problems with snakes either; I've trodden on them, I've had them strike me, I've had all kinds of incidents with snakes, but they don't worry me. More people get killed trying to kill snakes than those who simply walk away'. The approach of winter snow and the freezing of the lakes wound up their Canadian adventure and produced another complete change.

Newmont Mining executives in New York sent Hopwood into something of a lion's den, as an outsider consultant at the copper-lead-zinc mine at Tsumeb in South West Africa — at 5,800 feet (1,775 metres) one of the deepest base-metal mines in the world. Meg recalls: 'Tim was the meat in the sandwich — the outsider pushed into a mining community of five thousand people, most of them white'. (South West Africa, Namibia, won independence from South Africa during 1989 under United Nations guidance.) After the stint at Tsumeb, Meg pointed out that they had spent only six weeks of the last year in Adelaide 'and it was meant to be our home'.

Hopwood, too was 'getting sick of tramping round the world with suitcases', and resolved to change his *modus operandi*; instead of simply collecting fees, 'I decided that the next discovery I was involved in would give me some percentage of the equity'. He and Meg had, in fact, been able to assemble capital in their travels. 'We used to take the money and invest it, building a capital base.'

Not that their outback travels were over. As well as working up and down Australia, they made three visits to the vast kingdom of Saudi Arabia which has a larger land area than western Europe. As a result of the oil embargo in the early 1970s, the Saudis were incredibly rich — a national income of *$300 million a day*, which was roughly $300 for every male Saudi every day (the females don't tend to count for much in that society). They were anxious to diversify from oil (although they have far-and-away the biggest oil deposits in the world) so Hopwood was engaged by Saudi and British joint venturers to seek for gold and base metals. The London executives were against Meg going too, saying they could not guarantee her safety. Hopwood told them: 'Meg comes or you don't get me.'

In fact, Meg had a fascinating time among the Bedouin in the desert — for they were operating away from the roads, simply following map references across the sand: 'We always believe that you have to fit in with local custom. I always wore a long dress, long sleeves and a scarf. When we arrived at a camp, Tim went to see the local head-man and I went off to the women's tent. We had no language together, so they looked at me and I looked at them. Underneath their black garments of purdah, they were wearing the latest fashions — high-heeled shoes, gold bracelets, garish brocade dresses — despite the hot climate. Because I was a woman, they were proud to take off their outer garments and show me what they had on underneath.'

The full complement was a Somali cook and an Arab driver in addition to the Hopwoods, and they navigated from photo-mosaic maps. Over a total of twelve months, Hopwood looked at some four hundred prospects in Saudi Arabia 'and about twenty were worth a full investigation, say 5 per cent. I actually picked up gold that assayed at 640 grams, the richest I've ever found.' (Hopwood is sure that Sir Arvi Parbo got it right when he said: 'Geologists *must* be optimists. If a geologist does not believe he is going to find an orebody next week or next year, it is an impossible life for him. He must believe that there is ore hidden somewhere out there and that he is going to find it.')

Between trips to Saudi Arabia, Hopwood was learning how to be an entrepreneur, getting a better understanding of corporate systems and the mechanics of capital raising; he also assessed properties for possible development. One which occupied his attention was the Cracow mine, a gold and silver operation on Queensland's Golden Plateau about 130 miles (200 kilometres) inland from Bundaberg, the State's sugar capital. Eventually he floated Cracow Gold Limited and it secured an eighth share (12.5 per cent) in the Cracow Mining Joint Venture in which Costain, the British construction people, had 50 per cent. It produces about 40,000 ounces of gold a year at 4.5 grams of gold per tonne of ore from an open-cut mine. An exploration venture in northern Queensland resulted in the discovery of a major deposit of kaolin — the fine white clay used as a finish to high-quality paper — near the Skardon River just 80 miles (130 kilometres) from the northernmost tip of Cape York. This was floated as Venture Exploration NL and is now being actively developed. Hopwood is currently chairman or a director of five public and four private companies, all concerned with aspects of mining.

It was in 1984 that he became interested in Synroc: 'I was aware of it — I'd read Ted Ringwood's book and the early report in *Nature* — and I saw Synroc simply as a risk venture. Enquiries showed that the thing was languishing, which I found pretty pathetic for what I considered a very substantial invention addressing a significant problem.' Hopwood talked with

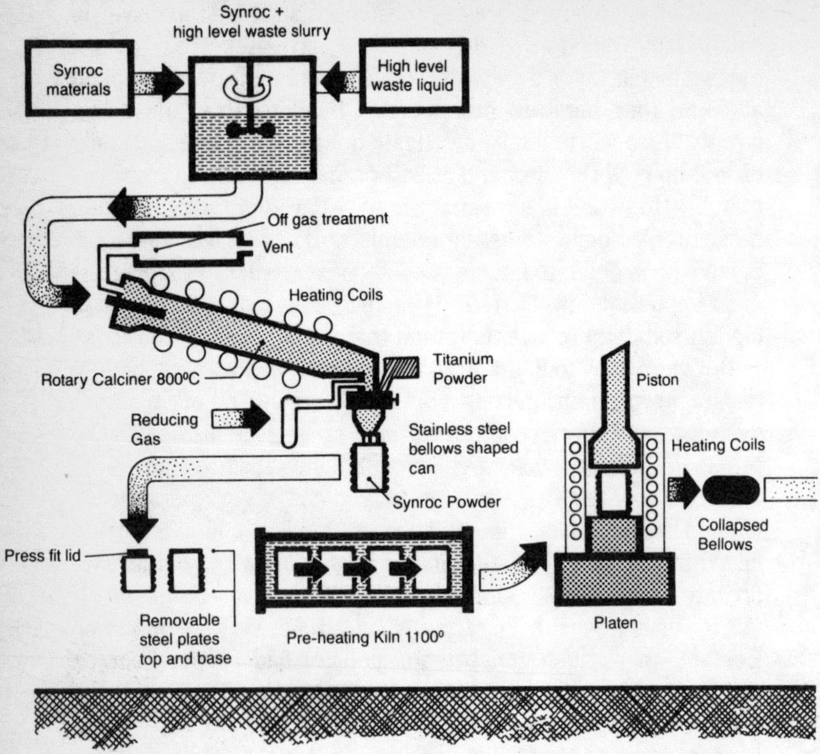

The Synroc approach — from raw waste to safe keeping

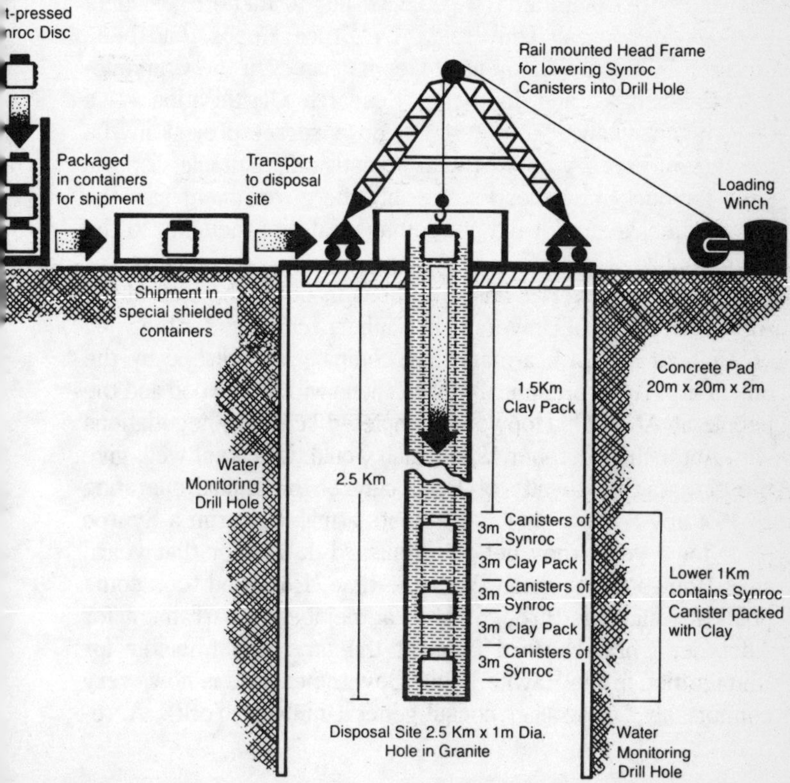
t-pressed
nroc Disc
Packaged
in containers
for shipment
Transport
to disposal
site
Rail mounted Head Frame
for lowering Synroc
Canisters into Drill Hole
Loading
Winch
Shipment in
special shielded
containers
Concrete Pad
20m x 20m x 2m
1.5Km
Clay Pack
Water
Monitoring
Drill Hole
2.5 Km
3m Canisters of Synroc
3m Clay Pack
3m Canisters of Synroc
3m Clay Pack
3m Canisters of Synroc
Lower 1Km
contains Synroc
Canister packed
with Clay
Disposal Site 2.5 Km x 1m Dia.
Hole in Granite
Water
Monitoring
Drill Hole

Ringwood who he found 'pretty disillusioned at that time — he had talked with more than seventy Australian companies and could not find any risk backing for Synroc. He had taken the thing to America but he could not beat the glass boys.'

Hopwood was inclined to give Synroc his best shot. He launched Nuclear Waste Management, a private company, by putting in loan funds of $350,000 out of his own pocket. He drew up a three-pronged business plan: '1. To acquire a licence to the basic Synroc patents; 2. To gain a source of high level nuclear wastes for construction of an active Synroc plant, and 3. To gain an agreement for a disposal site for high level nuclear wastes immobilised in Synroc.'

His entrepreneurial interest was undoubtedly boosted by the knowledge that another top geologist and former Professor of Geology at Monash University, Dr Bruce Hobbs, had been engaged by the Department of Geomechanics in the Commonwealth Scientific and Industrial Research Organisation — a government-financed outfit — to do a secret project in the Northern Territory of Australia: investigating suitable disposal sites for nuclear waste! Presumably the government saw the possibilities, even if it did not communicate its thoughts to the voting public.

Patented discoveries and inventions made by the staff of the Australian National University in Canberra come under the wing of Anutech Pty Ltd, a marketing company established by the university. After preliminary discussions with Ringwood and the people at ANSTO, Hopwood completed licensing negotiations with Anutech in October 1985 which would, if all went well, give the university a royalty of 1 per cent of the annual operating cost of any Synroc plant. 'If it costs a million to run a Synroc plant for a year, they get ten thousand dollars for that year,' says Hopwood. At much the same time, Hopwood took some political soundings through his local member of parliament for Adelaide, Chris Hurford (who at the time was Minister for Immigration in the Hawke Labor Government and is now, very comfortably, Australian consul-general in New York). A response is on the record from Senator Gareth Evans, the then Minister for Resources and Energy:

> Should the promise of Synroc as a second-generation waste immobilisation method be fulfilled . . . I see no reason why Australian firms should not seek to participate in the commercial development of Synroc *in overseas countries.*

I have added the italics. The letter went on (notwithstanding Dr Hobbs' investigations in the Northern Territory):

> The Government is opposed to the importation, for disposal in Australia, of radioactive wastes from the back end of the nuclear fuel cycle. These considerations make it extremely unlikely that the Government would support the construction of an active [as opposed to the inactive pilot at Lucas Heights which did not handle real nuclear waste] Synroc plant in Australia.

This is so typical of what Hopwood — and other frustrated nuclear people — calls the Nimby Syndrome: Not In My Backyard, which we have struck before. The fact is that Australia is ideally suited to becoming the permanent home for high level nuclear waste. The empty acres of the interior of the old island continent — half a million square miles, still much less than 20 per cent of the whole and five-and-a-half times the area of the United Kingdom, three times the size of California, more than twice France, almost twice Texas — this semi-desert is geologically perfect for deep burial of Synroc-contained waste and there are only handfuls of people out there. The receipts from becoming such a graveyard would solve in one hit the country's chronic imbalance of imports over exports. But, given the phobia about nuclear power, no government of either left or right is prepared to discuss the concept, let alone tackle the enlightened task of educating the people that nuclear power is not only safer but utterly required to save the human race and that nuclear waste can be coped with.

But I digress.

Hopwood went on a fact-finding tour 'to gain a perspective on the nuclear waste disposal industry and the reaction of the industry of Synroc, and to define opportunities for its application'. It took him to Europe, Scandinavia and North America to visit various establishments and attend three international conferences. He ran into a bewildering wall; the concensus was 'glass is good enough', even from scientists who knew that, long term, glass is no good at all. Further, he was warned more than once not to be critical of glass. Dr Richard Gurley, of Rockwell at Richland in Washington state, told him that glass was too well established, adding: 'The train has left the station and Synroc isn't on it — and it's a big train.' (Warnings against giving the facts about borosilicate glass have persisted; late in 1988 Hopwood received a letter from a senior man at Marubeni in Tokyo, a Y. Itoh, telling him not to show 'a negative attitude toward the existing technology' and suggesting, no doubt with the best intent, that he 'observe the rule of the game if you wish to be a member of the game, otherwise you can never even get a card'.) Hopwood did pick up some encouraging signals. At his first landfall, in Stockholm, Hans. S. Carlsson, the director of nuclear waste management at SwedPower, told him unequivocally that Synroc technology was far superior to glass and in his role as a consultant he would recommend Synroc to clients. Then from Professor E. Merz he heard that a team led by Armid Solomah at the professor's institute at Julich in West Germany had used fast-reactor waste to test Synroc and it had worked beautifully; Merz said he had been retained by the 'German government to find out whether Ted Ringwood's claims for Synroc were fact or fantasy and he concluded that they were absolutely correct and that Synroc was better than glass. (Pressure from supporters of glass eventually led to the termination of Merz's research grants, on the grounds that 'German government policy was to vitrify'. And at an international conference on waste organised by the Canadian Nuclear Society in Winnipeg, Dr John Shade, a research chemist at Battelle Laboratories in the United States, said that their tests involving powder rather than big blocks had shown that 'Synroc was one hundred times less leachable than glass'.

Perhaps the strongest endorsement of all came considerably

later, in 1988, in the book *Radioactive Waste Forms for the Future*, edited by Werner Lutze, of the Hahn-Meitner Institute in Berlin, and Rodney C. Ewing, of the University of New Mexico at Albuquerque, which focused on the two most 'extensively characterised waste forms; borosilicate glass and Synroc'. It concluded that glass corrodes too quickly under water and Synroc does not, and offered this chilling comment: 'Long-term containment of the more soluble radionuclides in such a glass is impossible.'

At that conference in Winnipeg Dr Maurice Giniff, a British scientist involved with low-level waste, related how people say to him: 'The problem with radioactivity is that you can't see it, feel it or smell it and that it could kill you.' And how he replies: 'Gravity is something you can't see, feel or smell, and yet a lot more people have been killed by gravity than by radioacitivity.'

Hopwood found a three-day conference on waste at the Uranium Institute in London the most depressing, for the Institute is the real home of 'glass is good enough'. He recalls: 'It is a club for uranium producers and users and it is dominated by executives of large corporations who are coming to the end of their careers. If you go back every couple of years you observe the change in membership. The last things the members want to do is make decisions. They say that, with glass, decisions can be deferred for thirty to fifty years as it is satisfactory interim storage — they forget that the first thirty years have already run out.'

Hopwood found, too, as Ringwood and indeed Sir Edward Bullard had done earlier, that the wrong people were making the decisions — or failing to make decisions. 'The ultimate disposal of nuclear waste relates to the chemistry of materials within the earth's crust. These wastes are going to remain thermally hot for 600 years and they are going to be radioactively hot for at least 10,000 years. Some people say it should be 100,000 years or more, but it's a minimum of 10,000', says Hopwood. 'There are not many groups of professionals who are used to dealing in those kinds of time frames, only geologists and people in the earth sciences are. Engineers, by and large cannot think in those terms; and most of the people in the nuclear power business are essentially engineers and they are mostly concerned with plant. You talk of time frames of even a thousand years and their eyes glaze over.'

He was further dismayed that so many of the papers delivered at the international conferences — on subjects ranging from water-flow studies to safety — were computer modelled with little and in some cases *no* hard data; he noted: 'There is a deplorable and myopic tendency in the nuclear-disposal industry to blind themselves with erudite computer models unsubstantiated by significant and abundant data.'

Despite many daunting omens, Hopwood returned to Adelaide and Nuclear Waste Management with confidence still high. He told his fellow directors: 'My view is that past approaches with Synroc have been nice enough for long enough. We have to be much more persuasive. Decision-makers will eventually be forced — through long-term frustration by the Nimby Syndrome, civil and state litigation and growing political opposition to specific sites in or near high-density populations — to concede that Nuclear Waste Management's plans for Synroc disposal in deep drill-holes in a third host country may be their only viable route.'

The question was: Which host country? For it must be recognised that several industrialised nations had targeted Third World nations as dumping grounds, not for nuclear waste but for the mountains of general waste that were being produced; the Third World responded with taunts of 'toxic terrorism' and 'garbage imperialism', and in due course some of the African nations set up a Dump Watch to monitor the situation.

In the campaign to become more persuasive, Hopwood turned to communications experts to produce material which could be widely understood, as opposed to learned journals which were read almost-exclusively by academics; they produced a colourful thirty-page brochure which said simply on the cover: 'Synroc is the safest and cheapest option available for disposal of high-level nuclear waste'. More than that, the senior consultant involved, Mark Kerr, had been to China on other business and was sure the Chinese could be interested. Indeed, they had offered as far back as 1983 sections of the Gobi Desert — sandy wastes traversed by Marco Polo in the thirteenth century — in Mongolia as a nuclear waste storage site for developed nations, an offer repeated in 1985 to West Germany which had lots of spent fuel and 850 tonnes of high level waste it did not know what to do with; *Nucleonics Week* reported that China would take permanent title to the spent nuclear fuel at a fee 'in the neighborhood of $1,500 a kilogram' — good money for a nation badly wanting hard currencies.

To have useful negotiations with the Chinese it is usually advisable to work through someone who has spent years in the country and established trust. Such people form a foyer culture and they can be seen in capitals throughout the developing world, notably very big capitals like Beijing or very rich ones like Riyadh; they are vital in oiling the wheels of commerce. MaeCile Eastin (the singular way of spelling her given name sprang from a tradition within her family in the southern states of America) has toiled in Beijing for seven years, first at learning the language and at making contacts, and then at making introductions for outsiders; her headquarters is a suite in the Xiyuan Hotel. Mark Kerr introduced Hopwood to MaeCile and MaeCile introduced him to Yang Liji, chief engineer in the division of waste management in the Beijing Institute of Nuclear Engineering. In the northern summer of 1988, the introductions broadened to include Zhao Liang of the Institute and three senior executives of the China National Nuclear Corporation: Jiang Yun-qin, Jin Youcai and Zheng Hualing. Negotiations opened with Hopwood and Kerr on the one hand and Jiang Yun-qin and Yang Liji on the other with MaeCile in the middle; 'friendly discussions' led to Hopwood, Jiang and Yang signing a Letter of Intent on 17 August 1988 to develop a feasibility study 'to construct an active Synroc demonstration plant and disposal respository in the People's Republic of China.'

A remote tentative site was identified just to the east of the Gobi at a place called Yiauyaguan, already served by a railway. For his eventual contribution to the feasibility study, Hopwood turned to Costain Engineering in England (their Australian arm already had an equity interest in Nuclear Waste Management); they had all kinds of valuable experience in nuclear design and construction, in waste encapsulation (in glass) and in working with the Chinese — they had built a conventional power station in the People's Republic. A three-man Costain team — John Yarnall, Tony Kay and Mike Myall — were soon in Australia, working with Hopwood and visiting Lucas Heights.

Clearly there will be further negotiations in Beijing — complicated, no doubt, by events in Tiananmen Square in May–June 1989 — and, once under way, the feasibility study would take at least six months. But it was a start, indeed a significant start. And to buoy up his spirits, Hopwood has other positive expressions of interest for another source of wastes and a disposal site from the Soviet Union. Other (Western) countries have also expressed interest.

Chapter

13

Solving the Head Problem

We all have to be greenies now — not least because, as a conference of hundreds of climatologists and atmospheric scientists decided in Toronto in June 1988, the mixture of the Greenhouse Effect, the Hole in the Sky and Acid Rain could easily have a consequence 'second only to a global nuclear war'. As Margaret Thatcher said to the Royal Society (of which she is a proud member, having been a research chemist before going into politics) in October 1988: 'We may have unwittingly begun a massive experiment with the system of the planet itself.'

But we do not have to be like the greenies of yesterday. Indeed not. For they were, for the most part, special interest groups — not elected by anybody and not answerable to anyone — who gave off an air of extremism and intolerance and were opposed to any industrial development or economic growth whatsoever; they did not mind, either, breaking the law and implying that they had a special right to do so.

The need for everyone to become a constructive conservationist has been recognised at the highest level, by the

Thatchers, Bushes, Mitterands et al. (And Gorbachev gave the thing a twist while visiting London in the northern spring of 1989, by announcing that the Soviet Union would stop processing uranium for weapons, although they remain wedded to nuclear power generation.) And we have considered the spate of conferences on a series of questions from the Greenhouse Effect through CFCs to trading in waste which show clearly that the formal world — governments, bureaucrats, scientific bodies — is responding quite seriously to big challenges.

So too, in some directions, is the private world of the individual in which toilets are set at half-flush, gardens are composted with shredded newspapers and re-cycling is the mode for almost everything. The magazine *Good Weekend* sought suggestions from its readers for saving the planet and was 'overwhelmed'; some ideas: slap a tax on all plastic containers; use cloth nappies instead of disposable ones; avoid buying canned food — including dog meat in tins; a deposit-on-return system should be introduced to re-cycle bottles — specially beer bottles; do a bit of walking for a change and use the car less: And, 'assume a married couple lives for three generations, each of 25 years; if the couple abstain from having their three children then they would have contributed to a 60 per cent reduction in the people-equals-consumption-equals-pollution pattern for their first 25 years; a 79 per cent reduction in their second (assuming the birth rate of three for each generation); and a whopping 89 per cent reduction by the time they died', from R. W. Adams. (Incidentally, 61.3 per cent of the suggestions carried female signatures; perhaps women are more planet-minded than men.)

In fact, all kinds of people were addressing the problems and coming up with solutions. In its deep and thoughtful coverage of 'Endangered Earth' in its Planet of the Year edition, *Time* spelled out a five-point program in response to the problem: 'Greenhouse gases could create a climatic calamity':

- Impose special taxes on carbon-dioxide emissions.
- Provide financial aid to developing nations to build high-efficiency power plants.

- Launch a mammoth international tree-planting program.
- Develop techniques to recover methane given off by landfills and cattle feedlots.
- Increase funding for research on alternative energy sources, including solar power, and safer designs for *nuclear reactors*. (italics added)

It is those last words which are so vital. The nuclear phobia persists and somehow it has to be cured if we are going to stand a chance. I was much interested a few months ago by a lecturer called Jeremy Leggett who sent a piece headed 'How do you rate the end of the world?' to *New Scientist* (5 November 1988). He said that he talked to his thirty-six second-year geology students about what all the earth-warming fuss is about and then asked them to complete a short questionnaire.

The first asked whether they shared the opinion of the United Nations Commission on Environment and Development that 'global environmental change seriously threatens the future of mankind?' 82 per cent said Yes. 18 per cent did not know. No one said No.

Then: 'In the light of the conclusion that the burning of fossil fuels must be cut if global warming is to be slowed, I asked the students whether they thought that there was no choice but to expand nuclear power programs. Fully two-thirds said No.' The next question was: 'Do you believe that the nuclear program can operate into the future without potentially life-threatening accidents?' 39 per cent said Yes, 45 per cent said No and 16 per cent did not know. Among these bright young people, of those who had an opinion, 47.6 per cent believed nuclear programs can operate safely, yet 66 per cent-plus were against following that opinion.

It is interesting to compare those attitudes with the views of established academic scientists in the United States. Professor Cohen, whom I have cited two or three times before, conducted a poll by mail among 'the community of radiation health scientists' restricting it to 'those employed by universities, which reduces the suspicion that their opinions are influenced by the security of their employment and selects those more likely to be close to research'. Of the 211 responses he received, 74 per cent were furnished by people holding doctorate degrees. Perhaps the most interesting question read:

> In comparing the dangers of radiation from a nuclear power industry (at least 50 per cent of all electricity generated by nuclear power plants) with the dangers of air pollution from a full coal-powered industry, including accidents as well as routine operation in both cases, which of the following represents your views?

	Number of answers	*Percentage of answers*
Nuclear is grossly more dangerous	7	3.44
Nuclear is substantially more dangerous	10	4.93
Nuclear is slightly more dangerous	21	10.34
The two are roughly equally dangerous	31	15.28
Coal is slightly more dangerous	40	19.70
Coal is substantially more dangerous	79	38.92
Coal is grossly more dangerous	15	7.39
Total	203	100.00

Thus, after eliminating those who saw the dangers as about equal, 80 per cent of the involved scientists see coal as more dangerous than nuclear, to greater or less degree! Another interesting set of responses came to this question:

> In comparing the general public's fear of radiation with the actual dangers of radiation, I would say that the public's fear is . . .

	Number of answers	*Percentage of answers*
Grossly less than realistic (not enough fear)	2	.95
Substantially less than realistic	9	4.26
Approximately realistic	8	3.79
Slightly greater than realistic	18	8.53
Substantially greater than realistic	104	49.29
Grossly greater than realistic (too much fear)	70	33.18
Total	211	100.00

Of the scientists, 91 per cent rate the public's fear of nuclear radiation as exaggerated. Yet in the popular polls, nuclear is vastly unpopular. Much of the blame must rest with the scientists themselves; they are just rotten communicators and they have lost their nerve. Dr Stephen Schneider, an executive of the United States National Centre for Atmospheric Research, thinks that nuclear power is certainly part of the answer, but he is apologetic about it: 'I don't want to come across as a pro-nuclear person, but nuclear power *per se* is not evil, it's not a bomb.' It is safe to say, I think, that it was no accident that *Young Einstein* became the cult film of 1989, first in Australia where it was made and then in America where it was given a huge release, because it was the mad-scientist thing all over again. Consider the scene between the young hero and his father, a small farmer:

'You see, Dad, I want to be a physicist.'

'What do they grow, son?'

'Physicists don't grow anything.'

'What's the use of them then?'

'They study the basic rules and laws of the universe.'

'You can study the basic rules and laws of the universe in the evening, after you've done the washing up.'

Young Einstein, talking later with his girl friend, offered the belief that 'if you can't trust your government, who can you trust?' The lack of regard for scientists is reinforced by a certain crassness inside the nuclear industry itself; how does it expect the public to respond to headlines like this: '80pc of US atomic reactors fail safety tests'? (28 March 1989). This concerned a report by the United States Nuclear Regulatory Commission which documented that, in defiance of deadlines going back to the early 1980s, twenty-three power plants failed to install display consoles to help reactor operators monitor the plant's safety status more quickly; thirteen plants failed to install instruments to check on core cooling; nine plants had not put in instruments to tell operators about conditions inside containment vessels, and sixty-three plants had not carried out a detailed review of their control room to discover if operators could cope with an accident, despite a deadline to do so by 1

January 1983! Clearly the nuclear industry needs to lift its game.

Added to all this, there is a well-orchestrated strategy of disinformation in which media — given that the risk of nuclear accident is a never-ending soap opera — are willing partners. In the midst of a lively flow of letters to the editor of the *Australian Financial Review* about the pros and cons of nuclear power in the Greenhouse situation, Bill Hare, of the Australian Conservation Foundation contributed a note about unidentified 'detailed analyses' which showed that nuclear power is more costly than the alternative of energy conservation. Correspondents leapt in with obvious relish to reveal that the Conservation Foundation had extracted its information from a study by Keepin and Kats at 'the impressively-named Rocky Mountain Institute, the creation of Dr Amory Lovins and his wife, two dedicated anti-nuclear activists from way back'. (Derek C. Hampson, 2 February 1989). He added: 'The writers have used the information available to them in much the same way as a drunk uses a lamp-post — for support rather than illumination'. Another correspondent (D. S. Stewart, 3 February 1989) wrote that Keepin and Kats' 'contrived and contorted use of quite untenable assumptions, coupled with many statements which are demonstrably at variance with the truth, simply demonstrate the extreme to which the anti-nukes are prepared to go'.

As in other matters, James Lovelock — our Gaia man — offers wisdom:

> Fear feeds upon ignorance, and a great niche was opened for fear when science became incomprehensible to those who were not its practitioners . . . It is no exaggeration to observe that once some curious investigator pries open such a niche, it will be filled by the opportunistic growth of hungry professionals and their predators . . . Consider the size and intricacy of the radiation-monitoring agencies, of the industry that builds monitoring and protective devices, and of the academic community that has radiation biology as its subject. If the strong public fear of radiation was dispelled, it would not be helpful to their continued employment.

The job of re-education is immense. People must learn and

demand, as Stephen Schneider points out, that nuclear power plants can be built which simply CANNOT melt down; we must learn and demand that nuclear waste can be stored satisfactorily, almost to the end of time — because we are now, for the first time, really entering the nuclear age. In a way, it should be familiar — as Lovelock explains in the last words:

> **The natural energy of the Universe, the power that lights the stars in the sky, is nuclear . . . If this is so, and if God's Universe is nuclear-powered, why then are so many of us prepared to march in protest against its use to provide us with electricity?**

Selected Sources

Recorded interviews with Dr Tim Hopwood, Dr Sue Kesson and Professor A. E. Ringwood.

Cohen, Bernard L. and Lee, I. S. *A catalog of Risks*. New York, 1979.

Cohen, Bernard L. *Before It's Too Late*. New York, 1983.

Cranbrook *et al.* House of Lords report on *Radioactive Waste Management*. London, 1988.

Cribbin, John. *The Hole in the Sky*. London, 1988.

Elkington, John. *Sun Traps*. London, 1984.

Grossblatt, Norman. (ed.). *The Effects on Populations of Exposure to Low Levels of Ionizing Radiation*. Washington, 1980.

Hall, Tony. *Nuclear Politics*. London, 1986.

Haynes, Viktor and Bojcun, Marko. *The Chernobyl Disaster*. London, 1988.

Kasperson, Roger E. *et al. Social and Economic Aspects of Radioactive Waste Disposal*. Washington, 1984.

Lovelock, James. *The Ages of Gaia*. Oxford, 1988.

Novick, Sheldon. *The Careless Atom*. Boston, 1969.

Ringwood A. E. *Safe Disposal of High Level Nuclear Reactor Waste: A New Strategy*. Canberra and Norwalk, 1978.

Ringwood A. E. and Kesson, S. E. *et al. Synroc* in *Radioactive Waste Forms for the Future*. North Holland, 1988.

Robert, Alan and Medvedev, Zhores. *Hazards of Nuclear Power*. Nottingham, 1977.

Taylor, A. J. P., *English History, 1914-1954*, Oxford, 1965.

Thomson, David. *The New Cambridge Modern History*, volume XII, *The Era of Violence, 1898-1945*. Cambridge, 1960.

Titterton, E. W. *Facing the Atomic Future*. London, 1956.

Weart, Spencer. *Nuclear Fear*. Boston, 1988.

Williams, Robert and Cantelon, Philip. *The American Atom.* Philadelphia, 1984.

Periodicals:
New Scientist, Nature, Economist — Britain
Scientific American, Time — United States
Business Review Weekly — Australia

Newspapers:
The Times, Financial Times, Guardian, Independent — Britain
New York Times, Los Angeles Times — United States
The Australian, Australian Financial Review, The *Age,* The *Herald* — Australia

Index